Travel Guide

WITH

VIE

JOHN HOSKIN AND
CAROL HOWLAND

NEW
HOLLAND

★★★ Highly recommended
★★ Recommended
★ See if you can

Sixth edition published in 2011
by New Holland Publishers (UK) Ltd
London • Cape Town • Sydney • Auckland
10 9 8 7 6 5 4 3 2 1
website: www.newhollandpublishers.com

Garfield House, 86 Edgware Road
London W2 2EA, United Kingdom

80 McKenzie Street
Cape Town 8001, South Africa

Unit 1, 66 Gibbes Street
Chatswood NSW 2067, Australia

218 Lake Road, Northcote,
Auckland, New Zealand

Distributed in the USA by
The Globe Pequot Press, Connecticut

This guidebook has been written by independent authors
and updaters. The information therein represents their
impartial opinion, and neither they nor the publishers
accept payment in return for including in the book or
writing more favourable reviews of any of the establishments. Whilst every effort has been made to ensure that
this guidebook is as accurate and up to date as possible,
please be aware that the facts quoted are subject to
change, particularly the price of food, transport and
accommodation. The Publisher accepts no responsibility
or liability for any loss, injury or inconvenience incurred
by readers or travellers using this guide.

Publishing Manager: Thea Grobbelaar
DTP Cartographic Manager: Genené Hart
Editors: Thea Grobbelaar, Carla Redelinghuys,
Nicky Steenkamp, Melany Porter, Jacqueline
de Vos, Brigitte Lee
Cartographers: Reneé Spocter, Luyolo Ndlotyeni,
Tanja Spinola, Nicole Bannister
Design and DTP: Nicole Bannister, Lellyn Creamer,
Philip Mann, ACE Ltd.
Picture Researchers: Shavonne Govender,
Colleen Abrahams

Reproduction by Hirt & Carter (Pty) Ltd, Cape Town
Printed and bound by Times Offset (M) Sdn. Bhd., Malaysia.

Keep us Current
Information in travel guides is apt to change, which is
why we regularly update our guides. We'd be grateful
to receive feedback if you've noted something we
should include in our updates. If you have new
information, please share it with us by writing to the
Publishing Manager, Globetrotter, at the office nearest
to you (addresses on this page). The most significant
contribution to each new edition will receive a free
copy of the updated guide.

Cover: *A café in the old town, Hoi An.*
Title page: *A set of water puppets represents a
microcosm of Vietnamese society.*

CONTENTS

1
Introducing
Vietnam

Vietnam is strikingly beautiful – a country whose very existence is dominated by water; monsoons, floods, rivers and seas.

Up and down the land, rice paddies – at varying stages of growth – create a kaleidoscope of greens. Watery ribbons of newly planted paddies reflect the mountains and women in conical hats complete the animated oriental Lowry tableau.

In the north, sailing junks have disappeared from **Ha Long Bay** – motors are so much easier for the fishermen and their families who live on board, but picturesque, slim slivers of boats driven by a single, foot-powered paddle, still skim the rivers and bays.

Splendid red- and gold-lacquered pavilions and pleasure gardens line the banks of the **Perfume River** in **Hue** as relics of the last imperial capital. Further south at **Nha Trang**, fishermen paddle out to boats in tiny, tarred basket-boats and fish with huge shimmering nets that turn to gold in the evening sun. In the **Mekong Delta**, dense palms crowd the banks of the narrow canals and little boys leap off flimsy bamboo bridges.

The streets in the cities, that were once a swarm of bicycles, now throb with the roar of motorbikes. Glass and steel towers, new joint-venture hotels and mini-hotels have shot up amongst the old shophouses selling electrical and electronic goods. Internet cafés have replaced photo labs and photocopy shops as trendy new businesses, and charming new restaurants and smart new **resorts** have also opened.

TOP ATTRACTIONS

*** **Ha Long Bay:** bizarre limestone rock sculptures.
*** **Temple of Literature:** Hanoi's most intriguing and historically significant pagoda.
*** **Water puppets in Hanoi:** unique to Vietnam.
*** **Hue Citadel:** the imperial city of Nguyen emperors.
*** **Imperial tombs:** the tranquil burial ground of Hue's Nguyen emperors.
*** **Hoi An:** a tranquil ancient trading port.
** **Fragrant Perfume Pagoda:** a series of shrines in a stunning location.

Opposite: *Thien Mu (Pagoda of the Heavenly Lady) built in 1660, in Hue.*

WHEN TO VISIT VIETNAM

Given the considerable regional climatic variation, there is no single best time to visit Vietnam. The later months are generally best in the south, particularly the coolish, dry months of December and January. The **north** is most pleasant in September and October, and March and April. Heavy rains fall in **Hanoi** in July and August, in **Hue** in September and October and in the **south** from June to August.

Today the country is rushing headlong towards **consumerism** – racing to catch up with other lands. The poor, hardy Vietnamese who have struggled and endured so much for so long are at last seeing their lives improve little by little.

Vietnam's young people – more than two-thirds of the population are under 30 – clamour for Western fashions, football, disco music and karaoke. But amidst these changes, the people tenaciously hold to their **traditional** values: the strength and responsibility of family ties, respect for elders, a reverence for education and scholarship and a deep-rooted politeness.

Pizza may have arrived, but Vietnam's delicious universal noodle soup (*pho*) is still served in steaming bowls in pavement cafés. Along the coast, giant shrimps are still grilled in sea salt and garlic and at **Nha Trang**, seafood and rice are still traditionally cooked in coconut shells.

For the visitor, Vietnam offers numerous unique experiences. Only in Vietnam can one see **water puppets** (colourful carved floating dolls) dexterously manipulated by underwater bamboo poles, or hear the soulful wail of the one-stringed *dan bau* instrument, the hollow whisper of the giant bamboo xylophone, the *lem trung*, and the howl of Hue singing, while floating on a boat down the **Perfume River**. Only in Vietnam can one chortle at the tragi-farcical musical theatre, *cai leung*. The Vietnamese are a nation of poets and singers, passionate in their love of bright colours and costumes. Surprisingly, considering their grievous experience of successive **wars**, the Vietnamese are openly friendly to foreigners and a disarmingly warm and emotional people, eager to welcome visitors to their country of which they are so proud.

Below: *The Mekong Delta is justifiably known as the nation's 'rice bowl', producing over half the country's annual needs.*

THE LAND

Vietnam is a long thin country stretching 3260km (2037 miles) along the eastern coast of the Indo-Chinese peninsula on the South China Sea. The Vietnamese visualize their country as a long thin carrying pole with two rice baskets: in the north the **Red River Valley**, in the south the **Mekong Delta**. At its narrowest it measures only 50km (30 miles) wide. It covers an area of 330,363km^2 (127,520 sq miles), roughly the size of Italy.

Vietnam divides into three distinct areas: the **highlands** and Red River Delta of the north; the **Truong Son Mountains** and coastal plains linking north to south; and the Mekong Delta in the south. These divisions are known as **Bac Bo**, **Trung Bo** and **Nam Bo**, which correspond to the former French colonial districts of Tonkin, Annam and Cochinchina.

In the north, running from northwest to southeast, is the area's most important valley. Known as **Song Hong** in Vietnamese, the Red River rises in China's Yunnan province and flows through northern Vietnam, where the delta, a flat triangular region of some 3000km^2 (1158 sq miles), which was once an inlet of the Gulf of Tonkin, has filled up over the millennia with alluvial deposits. A lush and fertile region, it is the ancestral home of the ethnic Vietnamese and location of the nation's capital, **Hanoi**.

In its central region, Vietnam forms a long thin crescent, fringed by a narrow coastal plain and backed by the Truong Son Mountains running from north to south. These mountains, which have several plateaux, are broken by west-east spurs that divide the coastal strip into valleys. In the southern part of the area are the **Central Highlands** (Tay Nguyen), some 51,800km^2 (20,000 sq miles) of rugged mountain peaks, extensive forests and fertile red soil.

The southeastern shoulder of the country is surprisingly arid, in certain places giving rise to sand dunes that might have been lifted from the Sahara. Dominating the southwest is the **Mekong Delta**, which covers an area of about 40,000km^2 (15,440 sq miles) and comprises a vast, flat

ROUND VIETNAM

A full north to south tour of the country is recommended for the first-time visitor. With a minimum of 15 days, an itinerary might include: Hanoi, the historic and present capital; Hue, the last imperial capital; Hoi An (near Da Nang), the ancient port of the Chams; Nha Trang, for its fine beaches; Mui Ne, a new beach resort; Ho Chi Minh City (Saigon) and the Mekong Delta. With a minimum of 10 days, and concentrating on the north, an itinerary might include Hanoi, Hue, Da Nang and Hoi An; a trip to the south may include Ho Chi Minh City, the Mekong Delta, Mui Ne, Da Lat and Nha Trang. Transport could be a combination of plane, car, bus and train. It is best to fly from Hanoi to Hue, and from Da Nang to Nha Trang, making the rest of the journey by hired car (with a driver), by tour bus or train. Main roads, such as Highway 1, which links Hanoi to Ho Chi Minh City, are continually being improved, but still remain below Western motorway standards.

Right: *Everyone's image of a tropical beach – Vietnam is perhaps less well known for its several coastal resorts.*

alluvial plain where no point is more than 3m (9ft) above sea level. The Mekong is the world's 12th-longest river, running 4200km (2625 miles) from the Tibetan mountains through China, Myanmar (once Burma), Laos, Thailand and Cambodia to South China Sea at Vietnam's southernmost tip. At the northeastern apex of this intensely fertile delta is **Ho Chi Minh City** (previously known as Saigon), the country's largest metropolis.

A number of **offshore islands** in the Gulf of Thailand and in the South China Sea form part of Vietnam's territorial claims, including the **Paracel Islands** and the **Spratly Islands**, for which sovereignty is disputed by several neighbouring countries.

Climate

Vietnam has a **tropical monsoon climate** with high humidity year-round. The two monsoon seasons – the northeast monsoon blows from November to April and the southwest monsoon blows from May to October – are rendered almost totally meaningless by regional differences governed by **altitude**, **mountain passes** that block the weather and the distance from north to south. Suffice it to say that annual **rainfall** is substantial (so bring along an umbrella), ranging from 120cm (47in) to 300cm (118in), with 90 per cent of the rain falling between May and November in most places.

In Hanoi temperatures average 16°C (61°F) in winter and 30°C (86°F) in summer. The hottest months are from

April to September, the coldest are from December to March and the rainiest are July and August.

In the south, the seasonal differences are defined more as dry and wet than cold and hot. Annual temperatures average 27–31°C (80–88°F), the hottest months being from March to May, the coolest being December and January and the rainiest from April to October.

In central Vietnam, coastal regions are subject to typhoons in the summer, the hottest months are from April to September, the coolest from December to April and the rainiest from September to November. The central highlands are noted for a cool, almost temperate climate right through the year.

> **LOWLAND LIFE**
>
> The Vietnamese are traditionally a lowland people. According to legend, they are descended from the dragon king, Lac Long Quan, who married a Chinese fairy princess, Au Co. When the couple separated Au Co took half of their 100 sons north into the mountains and Lac Long Quan returned with his remaining 50 sons to his watery domain.

Flora and Fauna

Originally, the entire Indo-Chinese peninsula was **tropical** rainforest. In 1943, Vietnam's forests totalled 13 million ha (32 million acres) – 42 per cent of national territory. By 1982 the forests had shrunk to 7.8 million ha (19 million acres), about 23 per cent of the land area, due to colonial policies, wars, slash-and-burn agriculture and rapid population growth. Through the efforts of the government's **reforestation** pro-gramme, it was estimated by 1999 that forests extended over approximately 28 per cent of the land, but of this, only 10 per cent remains as primary **rainforest**.

There have been other gains – the U-Minh forest in the Mekong Delta has largely been rescued from the ravages of chemical defoliants and it is now the world's largest **mangrove swamp** outside the Amazon basin.

The National Conservation Strategy calls for the creation of more than 100 **protected areas** in addition to the already existing 11 **national parks**. The most accessible of these

Below: *Despite the ecological devastation that occurred during the Vietnam War, over 700 plant species continue to add colour, including the delicate lotus flower.*

Right: *Over 17,000km (10,600 miles) of Vietnam's inland waterways are navigable, although not always all year round. The Mekong Delta is less prone to flooding than its Red River counterpart in the north.*

are **Cat Ba National Park**, occupying half a large island 30km (18 miles) off the coast of Haiphong; **Ba Be**, north of Hanoi; **Cuc Phuong**, southeast of Hanoi; **Bach Ma**, near Hue in central Vietnam and in the southern central highlands, **Nam Cat Tien** and **Yok Don**.

Vietnam's flora and fauna are also diminishing. The country boasts some 12,000 species of plants, many of which have commercial value such as hardwoods, medicinal plants and sources of resins. Fauna, which numbers 273 species of **mammals**, 180 species of **reptiles** and over 800 species of **birds**, is sadly declining as natural habitats are being destroyed. Among the larger animals endangered are elephants, rhinos, tigers, mountain leopards, black bears, deer and certain species of monkeys.

HISTORY IN BRIEF

More than perhaps any other people, the Vietnamese have forged their national identity through centuries of almost constant struggle against one opposing force or another. The principal **battles** have been against domination by China (Vietnam's huge northern neighbour from whom it derives much of its cultural influence), and against natural barriers in a gradual expansion southwards from an original heartland in the Red River Delta, across the mountain spurs of the central part of the country and into the extensive flatlands of the Mekong Delta. The fact that the Vietnamese have maintained a distinct cultural heritage speaks volumes for their strength of national character.

The precise origins of the Vietnamese are lost in the mists of **mythology**. It is known that the earliest human habitation in the fertile plains of the Red River Delta probably dates back to Palaeolithic times. The first discernible lineage with today's peoples, however, did not begin to emerge until the late Neolithic period, early Bronze Age, when the Phung Nguyen culture was centred in modern-day Vinh Phu Province, northwest of Hanoi, from ca. 2000 to 1400BC. The development of wet-rice cultivation and bronze casting in the Red and Ma river plains from about 1200BC, gave rise to the sophisticated Dong Son culture, best known for its elaborate bronze drums (on display in the History Museums, Hanoi and Ho Chi Minh City).

Chinese Rule

It is believed that the Lac Viets occupied the northern delta plains and that a kingdom called **Au Lac** existed, although its boundaries are unknown. Some kind of **feudal** union probably prevailed until local power was gradually eroded by incursions from **Nam Viet**, a kingdom founded in 208BC by the Chinese general Trieu Da, that extended over much of what is now southern China. The Lac lords continued to rule in the Red River Delta but as vassals of Nam Viet, which held sway over the area for a century, while remaining on uneasy and constantly shifting terms with China.

At the same time, China was becoming reorganized under the **Han dynasty** (206BC–AD220). In 111BC, the army of Han Emperor Wu Di defeated Nam Viet and succeeded in gaining control over the Red River Delta.

LEGENDARY PAST

The Dong Son culture is linked in Vietnamese traditions with the semi-legendary Hung dynasty (mythological dates 2879–258BC) and the kingdom of Van Lang. The founder of the dynasty is held to be Hung Vuong, the son of Lac Long Quan – the Lac dragon king who taught the people the technique of wet-rice cultivation. Irrigated rice fields were called lac fields and, according to Chinese annals, the people were identified as Lac Viets, whom the Vietnamese recognize as their direct ancestors.

1000 YEARS OF CHINESE RULE

During Chinese domination revolt only served to make life more difficult – forced labour, the burning of Vietnamese libraries, and ceaseless, burdensome demands for tribute were typical. An ironic reflection on the state of affairs is found in the name the Chinese gave Vietnam in the late 7th century – *Annam*, meaning the 'Pacified South'.

Below: *Java-influenced stone carving on display at Da Nang's Museum of Cham Sculpture.*

There followed nearly 1000 years of **Chinese rule**, when the Lac Viets were governed, with varying degrees of severity and resistance, as a province of China.

Although China's domination was prolonged and its cultural influence indelible, the Vietnamese never willingly accepted the situation. Several rebellions and uprisings during the millennium of Chinese rule took place, setting a historical pattern of mutual **antagonism** that has never entirely vanished. Forcible attempts to Sinicize the local culture were resisted, but the Lac Viets inevitably underwent permanent change while under the Chinese yoke. Exposure to **Confucianism** was particularly influential, and the later evolution of Vietnamese administration, law, education, literature, language and culture generally displays pronounced Chinese elements. The indigenous **culture** of the ordinary people was to a great extent preserved, but the ruling elite were profoundly affected and later maintained a deep admiration for Chinese culture which, nonetheless, always stopped short of willing acceptance of Chinese political control.

It is from such an involved history of socio-political evolution that Vietnam gradually developed its complex national character, partly moulded by Chinese cultural influences – Buddhist, Taoist, Confucianist – and partly by a powerful nationalist and militaristic force generated by the struggle for national survival.

Funan and Champa

Chinese sovereignty never extended be-

HISTORICAL CALENDAR

ca. 2000–1400BC Early Bronze Age Phung Nguyen culture.

1200BC Development of wet-rice cultivation and bronze casting.

208BC Foundation of the Kingdom of Nam Viet.

111BC Chinese gain control of Red River Delta from Nam Viet.

AD39 Trung sisters lead ultimately unsuccessful revolt against Chinese rule.

939 After defeat of Chinese, Ngo Quyen founds first national dynasty.

1009 Founding of Le dynasty; southward expansion begins.

1010 Capital moved to Hanoi.

1070 Founding of first university, the Temple of Literature in Hanoi.

1225 Tran dynasty succeeds Le dynasty.

1257, 1284, 1287 Mongol invaders successfully resisted.

1407–28 Renewal of Chinese domination after collapse of Ho dynasty.

1428 Late Le dynasty founded after Le Loi overthrows Chinese rulers.

1471 Conquest of Champa Kingdom finally completed.

1771–1802 Tay Son peasant rebellion marks end of Late Le dynasty and unification of Vietnam.

1802 Prince Nguyen Anh as Gia Long proclaims himself emperor of the Kingdom of Vietnam and is installed in Hue.

1862 Cochinchina created as a French colony.

1883 Central and northern Vietnam set up as French protectorates, named Annam and Tonkin.

1890 Birth of Ho Chi Minh.

1924 Association of Revolutionary Youth, later the Indo-Chinese Communist Party, founded by Ho Chi Minh to oppose colonial rule.

1945 Ho Chi Minh declares himself president of an independent Vietnam on 2 September. French refuse to give up colonial possessions,

leading to First Indo-China War (1945–1954)

1954 French defeat at Dien Bien Phu ends colonial rule. Geneva agreement provisionally divides country at 17th parallel. Ngo Dinh Diem takes power in South, ending hopes for peaceful reunification.

1960 Formation of National Front for the Liberation of South Vietnam (NLF) prompts increased US involvement and the start of the Second Indo-China War (1965–75)

1969 Ho Chi Minh dies.

1975 War ends with North victorious over South. Reunification follows.

1986 Official government policy of *doi moi* (new thinking) introduced.

1994 US lifts Vietnamese trade embargo.

1995 Full diplomatic relations established between Hanoi and Washington.

2002 Trade agreement ratified between Vietnam and US.

yond what is now northern Vietnam, and the southern and central parts of the country were subject, respectively, to a separate historical development under distinct civilizations.

In the south, the earliest non-Vietnamese civilization was the kingdom of Funan, centred on the Mekong Delta. Probably inhabited mostly by people of the **Mon-Khmer** group, Funan is thought to have been founded sometime during the 1st century AD, though evidence is scant and the only historical accounts are Chinese chronicles, the earliest of which mentions **Funan** in the 2nd century.

MISNOMER

The word 'Funan' is the Chinese mispronunciation of the word *bnam* (*phnom* in modern Khmer), meaning 'mountain'. It was not the name of the country, which is unknown, but rather the title taken by its rulers, *kurung bnam*, 'King of the Mountain'.

CHAMPA KINGDOM

Occupying coastal territory north of the Mekong Delta, and with capitals at Hue, Da Nang, Binh Dinh and Phan Rang, the Indianized Champa civilization first emerged in the 2nd century AD. It comprised four states: from north to south, Amaravati (Quang Nnam-Da Nang), Vijaya (Binh Dinh), Kauthara (Nha Trang) and Panduranga (Phan Rang). Each, in that order, ultimately fell to the Vietnamese in the course of 14 centuries. A largely maritime people, the Cham were culturally and linguistically close to the Javanese. The civilization, which peaked in the 10th and 11th centuries, has all but vanished today, remembered in a scattering of tiered brick towers and some exquisite stone carvings.

The records of a 3rd-century Chinese embassy give a physical sense of place: 'There are walled villages, palaces and dwellings. The men are ugly and black, and their hair is frizzy; they go about naked and barefoot. They are simple by nature. Taxes are paid in gold, silver and perfume. There are books and libraries and they use an alphabet.'

To the Chinese all foreigners were **barbarians** and this prejudice doubtlessly explains the unflattering description. But the Chinese mention of taxes, libraries and an alphabet implies cultural influences from India – historians recognize a pattern of 'Indianization' affecting most of Southeast Asia at this time. Such influence was intensified later when rulers came directly from India. One 5th-century Chinese source tells of bronze images of Indian gods, and describes the king as sitting in a classical Indian posture.

The extent of Funan's power is unclear; 20th-century excavations at Oc-Eo (thought to be the kingdom's major port, located near the Mekong Delta's west coast) suggest a seafaring people engaged in extensive **trade**. Aerial photographs taken in the 1930s revealed the sites of hundreds of Funanese settlements, along with traces of ancient **irrigation** canals. Funan eventually lost its pre-eminence and its territory was taken over by the pre-Angkor Khmer kingdom of Chenla, and subsequently by Angkor itself. The Khmer were later to be ousted by the Vietnamese, although Khmer Krom (southern Khmer) still inhabit parts of the Mekong Delta.

Central Vietnam also has its own distinctive early **history** as the realm of the once powerful Hindu Kingdom of Champa. Like Funan, Champa was an 'Indianized' maritime state, first rising to prominence in the late 2nd century AD in the region around what is now the town of Da Nang. It remained a powerful force in the region until it was conquered by the Vietnamese in the 15th century.

Independence from China

The end of foreign rule over northern Vietnam was signalled by the collapse of China's **Tang dynasty** at

the end of the 10th century AD.
So weakened, the Chinese occu-
piers were defeated in the battle of
Bach Dang River in 938, after
which the Vietnamese General Ngo
Quyen founded the first national
dynasty. There followed a brief
period of **anarchy** and then subsequent weak, and usually shortlived, reigns. It was not until 1009

that a firm government was established with the founding of the **Le dynasty**.

The first 100 years of the new Le dynasty witnessed
warfare not only with China in the north, but with
the Khmer and the Chams to the south. Despite the
conflicts, in 1070 the country's first university, the
Temple of Literature in Hanoi, was founded. Once
external threats had been dealt with, the second century
of Le rule was a period of relative **peace**, during which
the nation made considerable gains – administration was
reorganized, public works undertaken, and agriculture
was developed.

The Le dynasty also witnessed the beginning of
Vietnam's southward **expansion**, prompted by population pressure. In 1079, the Cham were forced to cede
their three northern provinces and Vietnamese peasants
began occupying formerly untilled lands, turning them
into rice fields. Thus a pattern was set for the long
march south that would eventually lead to the Mekong
Delta and, in the process, the final defeat of the Cham
and the Khmer.

In 1225, a lord of the **Tran** family replaced the Le
through marriage and founded a new dynasty
(1225–1400) under which the country was further
developed by improved **administration** and **land
reforms**. The Tran were also notable for their military
campaigns against the Mongols and the Cham.
Invasions by the Mongol armies of Kublai Khan were
successfully repulsed in 1257, 1284 and 1287. In the
14th century the Tran became engaged in wars against

Above: *Founded in 1070,
Hanoi's Temple of
Literature is said to have
been fashioned after a
temple in Shantung,
birthplace of Confucius.*
Opposite: *Cham temple
tower, Po Klong Garai,
near Phan Rang, central
Vietnam.*

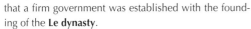

THE TRUNG SISTERS

In AD39 Trung Trac (the wife
of a Lac king who had been
executed by the Chinese)
and her sister Trung Nhi led
a revolt that held out against
the Chinese for two years.
When they were finally
defeated the Trung sisters
refused to surrender and committed suicide by drowning.
Celebrated as Vietnamese
heroines, they exemplify the
relatively high status of
women in Vietnam.

Above: *Pilgrims flock to Ho Chi Minh's Mausoleum, based on the design for Lenin's tomb in Moscow.*

VIETNAMESE DYNASTIES	
Ngo dynasty: 939–968	
Dinh dynasty: 968–980	
Early Le dynasty: 980–1009	
Le dynasty: 1009–1225	
Tran dynasty: 1225–1400	
Ho dynasty: 1400–1407	
Chinese rule: 1407–1428	
Late Le dynasty: 1428–1776	
(nominal after 1527)	
Tay Son rebellion: 1771–1802	
Nguyen dynasty: 1802–1945	
(nominal after 1883)	

the Cham and although they experienced both successes and reversals, the march south continued.

By the beginning of the 15th century the Tran dynasty had declined and was overthrown by the shortlived **Ho dynasty** (1400–07). In 1407, internal turmoil opened the door for renewed Chinese domination and the **Ming dynasty** ruled Vietnam harshly as if it were a province of China for the next 20 years.

In 1428 **Le Loi**, one of Vietnam's most celebrated heroes, liberated the country from Chinese domination and founded the Late **Le dynasty**. The country now experienced a golden age, particularly under the greatest of the dynasty's rulers, **Le Thanh Tong** (1460–97), during whose reign important administrative and land reforms were effected. The conquest of the Kingdom of Champa was also finally accomplished in 1471.

The Le dynasty degenerated in the 15th century and although it lingered until it was ultimately overthrown by the **Tay Son rebellion** in the 1770s, unified rule throughout the country was at best tenuous, as the power of the dynastic **monarchs** was diminished by rival clans competing for supremacy. From the 16th century onwards, two of these clans – the **Trinh** in the north and the **Nguyen** in the south – divided control of the country between them. During this time, with the Chams no longer a military force, the Nguyen continued Vietnam's southward drive, extending their influence into the Mekong Delta, where they wrested control from the Khmer and succeeded in establishing the southernmost limits of the nation by the late 18th century.

Arrival of the Europeans

Portuguese traders were the first Westerners on the scene, arriving in the early 16th century, followed by the **Dutch**. Trade contacts were shortlived, so European interests were left largely in the hands of **missionaries**, whose impact added a further dimension to the complexity of power struggles.

Predominantly **French** by the 18th century, the missionaries increasingly persuaded the French government to take a more political and military role in Vietnam in view of the unstable situation. The **Tay Son rebellion** (1771–1802) marked the final demise of the Le dynasty, as well as the overthrow of the Trinh and, temporarily, the Nguyen.

The rebellion, although initially successful, plunged the war-ravaged country into disarray, with factionalism persisting until the end of the 18th century. It was then that the one surviving Nguyen Lord, **Prince Nguyen Anh**, played into the hands of the future colonial power by seeking military aid from a French mission. He succeeded in raising an **army** against the Tay Son rebels, defeating them finally in 1801. A year later, Nguyen Anh changed his name to Gia Long, pronounced himself emperor of the Kingdom of Vietnam (the first use of the country's modern name), and installed himself in the Imperial City of **Hue**.

Under the **Nguyen dynasty** (1802–1945) founded by Gia Long, Vietnam was unified and ruled strictly according to the conservative, Chinese-influenced Confucian model. The absolute power of the government, however, was soon to be eroded by **French colonial interests**. Gia Long had rewarded French traders for their assistance during the Tay Son rebellion, but his successors reversed the policy and also took a repressive stance towards the European missionaries. This simply served to fuel France's growing involvement in the country.

Colonial Rule

In a series of military expeditions, beginning in 1847 at Da Nang, the French set about carving out a **colonial empire** in Indo-China. First southern Vietnam, Cochinchina, was formally created as a colony under direct administration in 1862 and subsequently, in 1883, the centre and northern parts of the country were set up as protectorates and respectively named Annam and Tonkin. A few years later the French consolidated

---

TAY SON REBELLION

Honoured as Vietnamese heroes today, the three Tay Son brothers led a peasant revolt in 1771 and took control of much of the country at a time of social dissatisfaction and near famine. In 1788 one brother, Nguyen Hue, proclaimed himself Emperor Quang Trang and led a famous victory against Chinese invaders. Quang Trang died suddenly in 1792, leaving the country in disarray once again.

NAME CHANGE

The name Vietnam translates
as 'the *Viet* people of the south
(*nam*)', and it was adopted in
the early 19th century by
Emperor Gia Long. He had
initially decided on 'Nam Viet'
but the emperor of China,
whose approval was sought,
feared it might be confused
with a similarly named
ancient kingdom, which had
included parts of China, so
he reversed the words to
Viet Nam.

effective control of the entire region with the creation
of the **Indo-Chinese Union** comprising Cambodia and
Laos as well as the three divisions of Vietnam.

Colonial rule brought some benefits – mainly in
agricultural and infrastructure development – but
mostly it sowed the seeds of discontent that would
eventually yield a bitter harvest. Higher taxes and
repressive rural landlords, in particular, served to
disrupt the traditional equilibrium of village life. Thus
the ground was prepared for **communism** to appear
as the only effective challenge to the French. Founded
and led by **Ho Chi Minh**, Vietnamese communism
preached a patriotic anti-colonialism policy and called
for a peasant revolution.

Communist opposition faced severe repression during
the 1930s, until **World War II** radically altered the
balance of power. Through an agreement between
France's Vichy government and the Japanese, a façade
of French colonial rule was maintained throughout
most of the war. But, in March 1945, the Japanese
deposed the French and installed **Emperor Bao Dai** as
head of a nominally independent Vietnam. Bao Dai
later abdicated in favour of **Ho Chi Minh** who, in the
early 1940s, had established the League for the
Independence of Vietnam, Viet Minh for short.

In spite of opposition from the Viet Minh, France
refused to give up the colonial possessions it had; in its
opinion they were only temporarily lost during World
War II. This led to a protracted war – the **First Indo-
China War** – which became another arena for the **Cold
War**, with China and the **USSR** backing the Viet Minh
and the **USA** giving financial support to France. On the
battlefield France suffered a humiliating defeat at Dien
Bien Phu in 1954, but peace talks in Geneva ended
inconclusively with the two sides agreeing to regroup
either side of a provisional ceasefire line drawn along
the 17th parallel. The French and the USA, however,
refused to sign political accords that would have provided for general elections. Vietnam had achieved
independence but effectively was divided into two

HO CHI MINH

Ho Chi Minh was born
Nguyen Tat Thanh to a
mandarin family in 1890 in
the northern province of Nghe
Tinh. After 13 years abroad he
returned to Vietnam in 1924
and founded the Association
of Revolutionary Youth, to
become the Indo-Chinese
Communist Party in 1930.
Later spells were spent in
Moscow and China. On 2
September 1945 he declared
himself president of an
independent Vietnam, so
beginning the nationalist
struggles against France and
later US-backed South
Vietnam. Ho Chi Minh
died in 1969.

countries, North and South Vietnam. When the intransigent Ngo Dinh Diem took power in the South, replacing Bao Dai, any hope of a peaceful reunification was dashed.

Diem's administration was particularly **repressive** against members of the Viet Minh who had stayed in the South, while his narrowly based policies in general alienated certain sections of the southern population, notably the peasantry and the Buddhists. The North (itself according harsh treatment to its dissenters) developed a strategy for involvement in the south and, in 1960, the National Front for the Liberation of South Vietnam (NLF) was formed to oppose Diem. This in turn prompted escalating US involvement in South Vietnam during the 1960s, first through so-called aid and finally through the commitment of combat troops. So began the **Second Indo-China War** – a well-documented episode of modern history. The dead (or missing in action) totalled 58,000 American personnel, 224,000 South Vietnamese soldiers, 1 million North Vietnamese and VC soldiers and nearly 4 million civilians – about 10 per cent of the population.

The tragedy ended in 1975 with the North's victory over the South and the subsequent reunification of Vietnam. The predicted bloodbath did not follow,

SYMBOLIC BRIDGE

Long Bien (Doumer) Bridge, the oldest of Hanoi's two spans across the Red River, became a symbol of resistance during the Vietnam War. Completed in 1902, the strategic 1682m (5519ft) bridge suffered nearly 200 sorties by US bombers but after every attack the Vietnamese managed to make repairs and keep the bridge open.

Below: *Lottery ticket vendors in Hanoi's old quarter. Vietnam's policy of renovation brings fresh economic challenges.*

although tens of thousands of officials, soldiers and other likely opposition were sent to 're-education' camps, some for 10 years and more. Huge numbers of **refugees** fled, some making desperate bids for freedom by fleeing Vietnam in small boats and many falling prey to pirates in the South China Sea. In an effort to halt the tragedy of the 'boat people', the USA set up an **Orderly Departure Programme** (ODP) which made provision for eligible political refugees (as opposed to economic refugees) to resettle in the West.

The Vietnamese government's attempts to rebuild the country after decades of war were slow. The first 10 years of peace under hard-line communist rule were largely a failure, and gains on social, political and economic fronts have been discernible only since 1986 when the government adopted a policy of renovation (*doi moi*). In the early 1990s the pace of change and **progress** began to accelerate at an unprecedented rate – limited only by a burdensome bureaucracy that has yet to be streamlined.

Below: *Sea products are an important source of foreign exchange. Leading exports are crude oil, garments and textiles, footwear, rice, pepper and coffee.*

GOVERNMENT AND ECONOMY

Following the Vietnam War, the Democratic Republic of (North) Vietnam and the Republic of (South) Vietnam were formally **united** on 2 July 1976, to form the present nation of the **Socialist Republic of Vietnam**. In broad colouring, politics are Marxist-Leninist and rule is dominated by the

Vietnamese Communist Party. In practice, government has been variously tailored to suit local needs and it has evolved to a certain extent in recent years.

Vietnam has had four constitutions, respectively adopted in 1946, 1959, 1980 and 1992, to suit prevailing conditions. These essentially display a waxing and waning of revolutionary communism, climaxing in the 1980 constitution, which defined the country as 'a state of proletarian dictatorship' and the Communist Party as 'the vanguard and general staff of the Vietnamese working class'. More than a decade of hard-line communist rule failed to yield economic gains and the 1992 constitution reflected **reform** and a more open-door policy, including privatization of state-owned enterprises.

Government comprises a nominally elected 500-member National Assembly, a Council of State, a sort of collective presidency, and a Council of Ministers that manages governmental activities. Changes brought about by the **1992 constitution** gave enhanced powers to the National Assembly, previously little more than a rubber-stamp organization, while the presidency was once again invested in an individual. Nonetheless, effective political power remains in the hands of the Communist Party, primarily with the 15-member **Politburo**, the party's highest policy-making body. With ongoing political reforms a shift in emphasis is discernible and, for example, there is now greater inner-party **democracy**.

The economy of Vietnam suffered greatly from the disastrous imposition of orthodox Soviet-style central planning. Accordingly, the country remains one of the world's poorest, with a per capita income estimated at $890 per year. The country's human poverty index (HPI) has declined significantly and is now lower than that of China, India or the Philippines. Only 12.3% (in 2009) of the population lives below the poverty line.

With the collapse of the Soviet Union, failure of the economic model was recognized in 1986 with the government's adoption of the *doi moi* policy of renovation, which resulted in continuing **reforms** and a gradual shift towards a market economy. In practice this has

TRADE FIGURES

Vietnam's major export markets are the USA, ASEAN countries, the EU, Japan, China and Korea. Following a meteoric rise in export growth averaging over 27% per year from 2005 through 2008, exports fell in 2009 by 9.7% to $56.6 billion – still representing 61% of GDP. But export growth is recovering. In the first half of 2010, export growth to the USA increased by 22% and by 21% to ASEAN countries. Following the US-Vietnam Bilateral Trade Agreement in 2001, exports to the USA increased a staggering 900% between 2001 and 2007. In January 2007, Vietnam joined the World Trade Organization, which released them from the restrictive quotas set out in the Agreement on Textiles and Clothing of 2005. In 2009, agriculture produced only 20.6% of GDP, industry 40.2% and services 39.1%, the industrial sector growing at a rate of 7.6%.

SOCIAL INDICATORS

Life expectancy: 74
Infant mortality: 12 per 1000
Fertility rate, average per woman: 2.6
Literacy rate: adults 94 per cent.
Telephones: 29.6 million lines, 70 million mobiles
Internet users: 20.8 million (240 per 1000).

Above: *Business is brisk in Hue's colourful Dong Ba Market.*

Below: *Agricultural methods have changed little over the centuries.*

meant decollectivization and the rise of the private sector, along with **foreign investment**. Vietnam's GDP rose to $92.4 billion in 2009, the growth rate falling back to 5.6 per cent from 6.3 per cent in 2008 and 8.5 per cent in 2007, supported in 2009 by growth of 1.83 per cent in agriculture, forestry and fisheries; 5.52 per cent in industry and construction and 6.63 per cent in services.

Inflation was brought down from a roaring 22.97 per cent in 2008 to 6.8 per cent in 2009, partly by the Government devaluing the currency three times, a total of 9.5 per cent. The country suffered heavy typhoon and flood damage in 2009, after which the government rebuilt or repaired 37,600 houses, sent 25,000 tonnes of rice to needy victims and directed $4.6 billion to support stricken localities.

Manufacturing has increased rapidly since the mid-eighties, particularly since 2000. Although Vietnam remains an agrarian society, agriculture, forestry and fishing occupy a dwindling 51.7 per cent of the population, accounting for only 20.1 per cent of GDP in 2009. In 2009 industry produced 40 per cent, services 38.7 per cent of GDP. Rice remains the major crop (Vietnam is the world's second largest rice exporter after Thailand) although rice only represents 5 per cent of the country's exports. **Farming** is still mostly unmechanized and the water buffalo continues to be the driving force. Other economically important produce include crude oil, apparel and textiles, footwear, seafood, agricultural products, coffee (Vietnam is the world's second largest exporter of robusta coffee after Brazil), wooden furniture, electronics, computers and handicrafts.

Since then exports have grown rapidly each year to reach a high of $62.7 billion in 2008, falling back to $56.98 billion in 2009, reflecting the world financial crisis. Domestic enterprises produced 53 per cent and foreign investment 47 per cent of total exports in 2009.

Rather surprisingly, Vietnam has added workers to its list of exports. In 2006, remittances through official channels from Vietnamese working overseas rose to a record $4.8 billion. In 2009, 467,000 Vietnamese workers were working abroad, of whom at least 171,000 lost their jobs, due to the world financial crisis.

Tourism has grown dramatically. From 2.9 million in 2003, in 2007 Vietnam greeted its 4 millionth foreign tourist. The first half of 2010 saw the arrival of 2.5 million tourists, and increase of 32.6% over the same period in 2009, most from ASEAN countries, Australia, the USA and France.

THE PEOPLE

Vietnam's total **population** is estimated at 85.8 million and increasing at an annual rate of 1.2 per cent. Slightly more than half (51.8 per cent) of the work force is involved in agriculture, primarily in the two main rice-growing regions: the Red River Delta in the north and the Mekong Delta in the south. Another 32.7 per cent work in services, 15.4 per cent in industry. Population density is high, an average of 260 people per km^2 nationwide, 932 per km^2 in the Red River Delta (excluding Hanoi) – amongst the highest in the world for a rural region. In the larger Mekong Delta, home to more than 17.2 million people, density is much lower at 425 per km^2.

The most populous cities are Ho Chi Minh City with nearly 7.2 million people, Hanoi with 6.5 million, and Haiphong with 1.8 million.

The vast majority of the people – some 85.7 per cent – are ethnic Vietnamese, the remaining 14.3 per cent made up of Chinese, Khmer, Cham and various ethnic minorities. Vietnam possesses a complex ethnolinguistic mix within its 54 ethnic minorities.

The pattern of minority

AO DAI

Charming among traditional cultural manifestations is the *ao dai* (pronounced 'au dzai'), the national dress of Vietnamese women made up of a close-fitting, high-collared, knee-length tunic in satin or silk with split sides and worn over wide trousers. Dating probably from the mid-18th century, but subject to changing styles, the *ao dai* is exceptionally attractive in its paradoxical blend of allure and modesty.

Below: *An evocative sight – non la conical hats, woven from latania leaves, are traditional Vietnamese head coverings.*

groupings is marked by a clear **ethnic** boundary in central northern Vietnam: to the north are mainly T'ai and Sinic minorities (T'ai, Tay and Muong tribespeople, among others), while to the south there are minorities belonging to the Malayo-Polynesian and Mon-Khmer language groups. The latter includes the lowland Chams and the Lat of the Central Highlands as well as the Khmer Krom of the Mekong Delta.

Most interesting of the minorities are the highland peoples (termed *montagnards* by the French), who are tribal people who preserve their own distinct languages, customs and beliefs. Living mostly in the northern mountain areas and the Central Highlands, the hilltribes have been traditionally regarded by the Vietnamese (historically a lowland people) as hostile and uncivilized. Until modern times the minorities have been effectively autonomous, but the semi-**nomadic** lifestyles and the environmentally destructive slash-and-burn **agriculture** practised by some tribal groups have promoted the government to encourage settled communities.

YIN AND YANG

Using the I Ching (Book of Changes) as its reference, **Taoist** belief stresses a cosmic view based on two contrary yet complementary forces – *yin* (female) and *yang* (male). In order for **harmony** to be maintained in life, a proper balance has to be achieved between *yin* and *yang*. Imbalance between these forces is believed to be the root cause of illness.

Language

The official language is Vietnamese (kinh), the mother tongue of the vast majority of the population and it is also understood by many of the tribal minorities. The most widely spoken European languages are English, French, and to a far lesser degree, Russian.

Vietnamese is related to the Austroasiatic family of languages, but has had a complicated evolution, having been influenced by Mon-Khmer and T'ai and classical

Chinese. The first two influences provided the basic vocabulary, while T'ai brought Vietnamese its **tonal structure**. Chinese provided literary and technical terms and also the language's first written form, which used variations of Chinese characters until a romanized script was adopted in the early 20th century.

As a monosyllabic and tonal language, Vietnamese can be difficult for the Westerner. Six tones are used in the north, five in the south, and every syllable is inflected by a tone, which determines the meaning. Thus words sounding the same to the untrained ear may have five (or six) different meanings.

Religion

Vietnam is ostensibly a socialist country but religious practice is permitted by the 1980 constitution, which states 'citizens enjoy freedom of worship, and may practise or not practise a religion'. Historically, the spiritual life of the nation has been moulded by **Buddhism**, **Confucianism**, **Taoism** and **Animism**, the latter being the earliest and most deeply rooted belief of the ordinary people. Most people call themselves Buddhist, although their faith will in all likelihood incorporate Confucian, Taoist and Animistic beliefs along with orthodox Buddhist teaching. **Catholicism** has had a significant impact since colonial times, while **Islam** is practised by the small Cham minority. Besides major world religions, Vietnam also has its own home-grown faiths, the **Cao Dai** and **Hoa Hao** sects.

Above: *Dazzling saffron robes are worn by Buddhist monks at Da Nang.*
Opposite: *The goddess of mercy, Thien Nan, with many faces and arms to see and serve the needy, Phap Lam Pagoda, Da Nang.*
Below: *Religious ceremony in Ho Chi Minh City. Ritual offerings are made to appease malevolent spirits of divinities, and to revere benevolent ones.*

Buddhism

Mahayana Buddhism has always predominated in Vietnam, brought to the Red River Delta by Chinese monks in the late 2nd or early 3rd century AD. **Theravada Buddhism**, which historically had a stronghold in Sri Lanka

ARRIVAL OF CHRISTIANITY

The first Western missionaries set foot in north Vietnam in 1533, but it was not until 1615 that the first Christian missions were founded by Portuguese Jesuits in Hanoi, Da Nang and Hoi An. Many Vietnamese converted to Catholicism, which the ruling classes viewed as a threat to the traditional order of society. In the north, a decree forbidding the practice of Christianity was enforced between 1712 and 1720, while in the south foreign missionaries were expelled and the religion outlawed.

and later spread to Myanmar (Burma), Laos, Thailand and Cambodia, is practised in parts of Vietnam, especially in the Mekong Delta, where it is the faith of the Khmer Krom minority.

Confucianism and Taoism

A philosophy more than a religion, Confucianism was brought to Vietnam by the Chinese during their 1000-year domination of the country. It emphasizes **duty** and **moral obligation** in social relationships within the family and society, and takes its cardinal virtues as diligence, economy, integrity and righteousness. Confucian society is essentially hierarchical and based on virtue, which may be acquired through education.

In Vietnam, Confucianism was important among the mandarin class and in the past played an integral role in shaping government, bureaucracy and social order. Deep-rooted remnants remain in the Vietnamese respect for elders, for the birth order within the family and for education.

Right: *Ho Chi Minh City's red brick and granite Notre Dame Cathedral, located in the government quarter, was completed in 1883. It is said to occupy the site of an ancient pagoda.*

Another Chinese import, Taoism follows the mystical philosophy of Lao Tze, which expounds a highly complex system of correspondences, stressing basically the value of a contemplative and simple life in harmony with **nature**. Throughout Vietnam's feudal history, there has been a tradition of mandarins retreating to the mountains to become philosophers or poet monks.

Christianity

Catholicism was first brought to Vietnam by European **missionaries** in the16th century. It suffered persecution at times but succeeded in establishing a solid position under **French** rule. In modern times, the faith has suffered from its association with colonialism and with the 1950s administration of President Diem in South Vietnam. Converts today probably number as high as 10 per cent of the population.

The Protestant religion was introduced to Vietnam in the early 20th century. Today, Vietnamese Protestants number 200,000–300,000, although restrictions were imposed on religious activities after the war in 1975.

Islam and Hinduism

There are very small numbers of Muslims and Hindus in Vietnam, nearly all of them belong to the **Cham** minority. Hinduism was an important influence on the ancient Kingdom of Champa in central Vietnam, and while many Chams converted to Islam after the fall of their civilization, Hindu elements remained.

Cao Daism and Hoa Hao

Founded in 1919 by a Vietnamese mystic, Ngo Minh Chieu, the Cao Dai faith is an idealized religion embracing a mélange of beliefs derived principally from Mahayana Buddhism, Confucianism, Taoism and Christianity, as well as a lacing of spiritualism.

One of the basic tenets of the religion is that it is the 'third revelation', following two previous eras of 'missionary saints' – a list that embraces the founders of the world's major religions. **Cao Dai** thus claims to supersede

---

ANCESTOR WORSHIP

A part of the **Confucian** cultural tradition, ancestor worship pervades religious practice throughout Vietnam. Not only are ancestors revered, the souls of the dead are also believed to survive and act as a family's guardian spirits. **Ancestor shrines**, today typically featuring photographs of dead relatives, are commonly found in Vietnamese homes.

or correct misunderstanding in earlier teachings. There is also a belief in the soul and in an absolute supreme god. Coexisting with the supreme deity are lesser gods and numerous contactable spirits (including Shakespeare, Victor Hugo and Lenin).

Another indigenous religion, the **Hoa Hao** sect is almost exclusively associated with the Mekong Delta, where it was established in 1939. Its founder, Huynh Phu So – dubbed the 'Mad Monk' by the French – was born at Hoa Hao village, near Chau Doc. At the age of 20, he began preaching a personal version of Theravada Buddhism after the allegedly miraculous cure of a persistent illness.

With currently more than a million followers, the Hoa Hao faith stresses individual **prayer**, simplicity and social justice rather than elaborate rituals.

Art and Culture

Unlike its Southeast Asian neighbours, Vietnam has a culture heavily influenced by China rather than by the region's other great civilization, India. Accordingly, whereas the traditional art forms of Laos, Thailand and Cambodia share certain common elements, the arts and architecture of Vietnam stand in marked contrast.

This fundamental **cultural** distinction is compounded by **historical** factors. The Vietnamese have never been great builders, as were the ancient Khmers, for example. Moreover, such has been the country's turbulent past that few of the significant buildings have survived.

Ironically, while Vietnam's political and social history has been one of expansion and struggle for freedom from foreign domination, its art history reflects mostly the influence of imperial China. Vietnamese vernacular **architecture** has developed in temples, pagodas, palaces and imperial tombs, made from stone, brick and wood. Buildings can be impressive although most have generally been renovated and remodelled numerous times, with the result that period styles are not always easy to determine. Geomancy and concern for harmony in arrangement and positioning were important

ART RENAISSANCE

Since 1987, when the Communist Party began to relax its grip on the arts, contemporary Vietnamese painting has experienced a minor renaissance. Some of the best work is to be found in Hanoi, where art galleries now abound. Prices, too, have soared from a few tens of dollars for a canvas to several hundreds, even thousands. **Modern artists** to watch out for include Nguyen Quan, Phan Cam Thuong, Nguyen Quang Huy, Nguyen Minh Thanh, Vu Dan Tan, Thanh Chuong and the Gang of Five (Hong Viet Dung, Ha Tri Hieu, Do Xuan Hoa, Tran Luong, Pham Quan Vinh) while current collectables include Nguyen Tu Nghiem, Bui Xuan Phai and Tran Luu Hau. For information call the Vietnam Fine Arts Association, 51 Tran Hung Dao, Hanoi, tel: 844 943 9594.

architectural considerations. In simple terms, **temples** and other major monuments tend to be squat, sturdy structures with thick, crusty roof tiles and a profusion of sculpted and carved ornamentation. The latter is often the most interesting aspect, and notably guardian spirits and other tutelary deities in painted or lacquered wood can be both beautiful and strikingly original. Nonetheless, the most distinctive classical art seen in Vietnam is not Vietnamese but that of the ancient Chams, who built tower-like religious monuments and produced some exquisite stone carving (best seen today in the **Museum of Cham Sculpture** at Da Nang).

Vietnam's decorative arts are highly developed, most obviously witnessed in temple decoration but also seen in traditional homes where carvings may adorn beams, partitions, windows and cornices – carpentry and carving are widespread skills. So, too, is the craft of making **lacquerware** (*son mai*), typically decorated with skilfully applied mother-of-pearl inlay.

Painting, both on canvas and on silk (a Vietnamese speciality), has in the past been a less accomplished art form than, for example, sculpture, in spite of silk painting dating back to the 13th century. In the modern age, however, painting has evolved remarkably and was given notable impetus during the French period. Social realism was the only acceptable art style under Ho Chi Minh, but with the greater freedoms of today, artists are able to exhibit work previously considered subversive, giving rise to a flourishing **contemporary art**, largely Western in form but Vietnamese in content, which is rapidly winning **international** acclaim.

Music and the **performing arts** have a long tradition in Vietnam and are closely allied in that theatre performances are always accompanied by an orchestra. Both have been heavily influenced by Chinese forms and, in the case of music, by Indian traditions via the Chams. Music and dance have also played an important part in both religious and court life. Vietnamese music has a five-tone scale and it is played on a variety of classical stringed instruments, flutes, drums and xylo-

Opposite: *Chinese, Vietnamese and colonial features are blended in My Tho's Vinh Trang Pagoda.*
Below: *A student learns the importance of poise in Hanoi's school of dance.*

phones. Although complex, much is easily accessible, but some not easily appreciated by the untrained ear.

Classical theatre combines **music**, **poetry** (a highly developed art in Vietnam) and **drama**. Hat Tuong is akin to Chinese **opera**, while older Hat Cheo folk theatre is less formal and depends a good deal on improvization for its characteristic anti-establishment **satire**. The more modern form, *cai leung*, which employs elements of both *tuong* and *cheo* and has farcical overly drawn characters, is quite easy to follow, without knowing a word of Vietnamese.

Water puppet theatre, unique to Vietnam, is highly entertaining and originated some 900 years ago as a folk art to accompany village festivals, when performances were staged on village ponds. This aquatic form of theatre features wooden puppets dextrously manipulated under water through bamboo rods, using a watery surface as the stage. Recently revived in Hanoi, water puppet shows based on peasant life and historical themes are performed daily.

Above: *Carved from water-resistant wood and painted in bright colours, water puppets may require as many as four people to operate them.*

Right: *The day's catch is ferried to morning market. Seafood features strongly in Vietnamese cuisine.*

Food and Drink

Although Chinese and French influences are discernible (French baguettes, for example), Vietnam has its own distinct **cuisine**, reputed to encompass more than 500 different dishes. **Rice** is the staple food and a typical meal comprises rice served from a communal bowl, eaten with helpings from other shared dishes of **pork**, **beef**, **chicken**, **vegetables**, **fish** and **seafood** (Vietnam's long coastline ensures abundant supplies). A soup is generally part of the menu and side servings of fresh raw green vegetables are also common. **Desserts** are typically sweet, such as sticky rice cakes and pastries, or fresh fruits.

Above: *Snakes are raised on farms and eating their flesh is believed to give men virile strength, so is drinking snake wine.*

The basic condiment is *nuoc mam*, a nutritious fermented fish sauce, a piquant flavouring and salt substitute. A spicier variation, *nuoc cham*, adds various ingredients such as chilli, lime juice, garlic and sugar to a base of *nuoc mam*. Other flavourings commonly used in Vietnamese cooking include lemon grass, basil, coriander and mint, as well as other spices typical of Southeast Asia. The food, however, is not especially spicy and while southern dishes tend to be hotter and make greater use of coconut milk than those in the north, many dishes are common to both regions.

Most typical of Vietnamese cuisine are **noodles** (*pho*), prepared as a soup with prawns, shredded beef or chicken. The Vietnamese eat noodles for breakfast, lunch or dinner – indeed, in villages, the traveller may find the dining choice limited to noodles. Another local favourite is spring rolls (*cha gio* in the south and *nem* in the north), fried thin rolls of rice paper stuffed with minced pork, prawn, crab meat, vermicelli, mushrooms and vegetables.

Drinks include **oriental tea** (usual with meals), strong coffee brewed from beans grown in the Central Highlands), imported and local **beer** (333 Export brand is a quite acceptable brew) and locally produced **wine** from Da Lat, which is quite palatable. Various local and imported soft drinks tend to be very sweet. Avoid drinking **tap water** or drinks containing ice.

READING THE MENU

fruit: *trai cay*
banana: *chuoi*
mango: *xoai*
coconut: *dua*
papaya: *du du*
bread: *banh mi*
coffee: *ca phe*
tea: *nuoc che*
beer: *bia*
mineral water: *nuoc suoi*
rice: *com trang*
vegetables: *rau xao*
(fried): (*hon hop*)
noodle soup: *pho*
beef: *bo*
chicken: *ga*
fish: *ca*
shrimp: *tom*

2
Hanoi

When Ly Thai To assumed power in the old capital, **Hoa Lu**, the way forward seemed clear: new dynasty – new capital. Guided by a heavenly vision, the first Ly emperor founded his new capital on a muddy alluvial plain in AD1010, creating first a royal enclosure, the Citadel, and then building city walls around it. The court drew in supporting craftsmen and the city grew. Throughout the next nine centuries, the court developed as a tight network of influential families whose scions rose as mandarins, constantly intriguing to seize power.

In spite of temporarily losing capital status to **Hue** during the 19th-century **Nguyen dynasty**, **Hanoi** is very much Vietnam's premier city. The French made it the administrative centre of their Indo-Chinese possessions, leaving behind a glorious architectural legacy in the city's many beautiful colonial villas and public buildings. North Vietnam was governed from here, and so is the reunified country today. For nearly half the country's 2000 years of history, Hanoi has provided the cultural force that has moulded the national character. As myths, legends and geomancy contributed much to the city's early planning, there is an appealing spirit of place about Hanoi.

Until fairly recently, Hanoi might have been considered a smaller, quieter, more traditional city than big and brash **Ho Chi Minh City** (Saigon). But in the past few years, Hanoi has rushed headlong into private enterprise and consumerism. New towers have shot skyward, new mini-towers (private homes and mini-hotels) have punctured the three-storey skyline, and battalions of

DON'T MISS

★★★ **Temple of Literature:** visit a fascinating temple.
★★★ **Old Quarter:** explore and enjoy Hanoi's traditional urban scene.
★★★ **Water Puppets:** see an art form unique to Vietnam.
★★★ **Vietnam National Tuong Theatre:** a burst of extravagant costumes and traditional music.
★★★ **Hanoi's Museum of Ethnography:** devoted to Vietnam's 54 minorities.
★★ **Ho Chi Minh's Mausoleum:** the memorial to Vietnam's modern architect.

Opposite: *Even in the Old Quarter, houses have added storeys and sprouted TV antennae.*

growling, bleeping motorbikes have replaced bicycles. Add now, a modern shopping plaza at one corner of Hoan Kiem Lake, a huge supermarket on the top floor.

Yet despite the recent rapid changes, with its lakes, tree-lined boulevards, venerable pagodas and French colonial architecture, Hanoi remains a genuinely attractive city with its own distinct charm. The palaces of the **Citadel** may be long gone, but the **Old Town of 36 Streets** – the quarter originally occupied by the craftsmen who served the royal court – functions to this day, and not much has changed.

ORIENTATION

With a population of 6.5 million, Hanoi sits like a spider at the centre of its web in the midst of the Red River (Song Hong) Delta. Hanoi is primarily located on the left bank of the **Red River** some 70km (44 miles) from the coast. The Red River is spanned by two bridges, beyond which much new urban development continues well past the right bank.

Central Hanoi is divided into four administrative districts: **Hoan Kiem**, the heart of the city in the northeast quadrant; **Ba Dinh**, in the northwest, site of the ancient citadel; **Hai Ba Trung**, stretching along the river bank south of Hoan Kiem; and **Dong Da** in the southwest quadrant. Most sightseeing is concentrated in the first two districts.

HOAN KIEM DISTRICT AND OLD HANOI

Turning its back to the omnipotent river, its banks devoted to unattractive earthen flood dykes, the city focuses on **Hoan Kiem** (Lake of the Restored Sword), the undisputed heart of the city, lying southeast of where the old Citadel once stood. It is on the banks of Hoan Kiem Lake where Hanoians collectively wake up in the morning, stretch their legs, wave their wooden swords to the sound of a transistor, kick a shuttlecock or wind through a t'ai chi routine followed by a bit of gossip – all before half past seven.

Ngoc Son (Jade Mountain) Temple **

On an islet at the northern end of Hoan Kiem Lake, **Ngoc Son Temple** (open daily 08:00–17:00) is noted for its pretty, tree-shaded location. Linked to the shore by a red wooden bridge named **The Huc**, which translates as the 'Flood of Morning Sunlight', the temple is relatively recent, dating from the late 19th century, and is dedicated to 13th-century national hero Tran Hung Dao – who saw off a 300,000-strong invasion dispatched by Kublai Khan in the 13th century – and

Above: *The island temple of Ngoc Son is reached across an arched wooden bridge over Hoan Kiem Lake.*

two illustrious scholars of his time. The temple gate is flanked by huge Chinese characters representing Luck and Wealth. Beyond is a stone tower topped with a calligraphy paintbrush (**Thap But**, or 'Pen Tower') and next to it is the writing pad (**Dai Nghien**). The chunky, pagoda-style buildings on the island create a romantic impression and this temple, along with Tortoise Pagoda in the middle of Hoan Kiem Lake, are undoubtedly the most frequently portrayed symbols of Hanoi – they are shown every evening on national TV weather forecasts.

Old Town of 36 Streets ★★★

North of Hoan Kiem Lake lies the old artisans' and merchants' quarter, an area of crowded, narrow streets and tiny, huddled shophouses. It was established in the 13th century by Hanoi's 36 guilds, each in a different street and each street named after the guild's function. 'Hang' translates as merchandise, therefore **Pho Hang Gai** means 'Silk Street' – of great interest to contemporary shoppers. **Hang Bac** means 'Silver Street', which today includes gold as well as silver jewellery. There were guilds specializing in wooden and china bowls, in string instruments, sandals, baskets, leather, mats, sails, brushes, thread, bottles, herbal medicine, incense, trays, hats, fans, coffins and bamboo. Among the most intriguing today are those devoted to red temple paraphernalia, votive papers (fake money for burning), tombstones and metal bashing – imagine listening to that din your entire life.

> #### MARKETS
>
> Dong Xuan Market is an inveterate browser's dream. Lying north of Hoan Kiem Lake on Hang Khoa Street, this is Hanoi's largest general market with stalls selling all sorts of things, from food and flowers to clothes, household goods, live animals and traditional medicines. Although Vietnam's economic focus has now shifted more to the west, you may still find inexpensive Russian caviar and vodka.

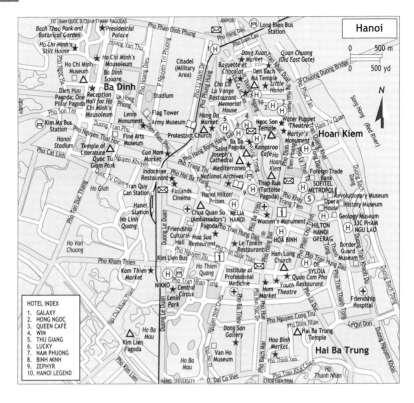

Hanoi

0   500 m
0   500 yd

N

HOTEL INDEX
1. GALAXY
2. HONG NGOC
3. QUEEN CAFÉ
4. WIN
5. THU GIANG
6. LUCKY
7. NAM PHUONG
8. BINH MINH
9. ZEPHYR
10. HANOI LEGEND

Den Bach Ma (White Horse Temple) ★

Located on Hang Buom Street in the Old Town, this well-preserved Taoist temple is dedicated to the spirit of **Bach Ma** (White Horse). It dates from the 9th century but has been repeatedly reconstructed, lastly in the 19th century. The story goes that the Ly Thai To, frustrated at his fruitless efforts to build the city walls (well, if you will build mud walls in a river flood plain...), came here to pray. His prayers were answered when a white horse appeared from the temple and lead him to where he should build the walls. The only remainder of his walls is the **Old East Gate**, still standing at the end of **Pho Hang Chieu**, a few streets away.

Water Puppets ★★★

The **Municipal Water Puppet Theatre** stands at the northeast corner of **Hoan Kiem Lake** and no visitor to Hanoi should miss a performance of this irresistible art form, unique to Vietnam. Originally a folk art that began in village ponds as early as the 10th century, the light wooden figures are manipulated through long bamboo poles under water. They perform the most incredibly dextrous feats, drawing from scenes in history, mythology and village life, accompanied by traditional music and singing. Daily performances – go and buy your ticket a day in advance.

Tuong ★★

You can now enjoy an amusing (one-hour) introduction to Vietnam's traditional opera based on myths and legends, music and dance at the new **Vietnam National Tuong Theatre** (51 Duong Than, tel: 4 834 0046, 4 764 3449, vietnamtuong@vnn.vn www.vietnamtuongtheatre.com Open Wed and Thu 17:00). Wildly extravagant costumes and kids love it. Brief explanations in English.

Cai Leung ★★

The **Cai Leung Theatre** in the old town stages what might be termed **Vietnamese musicals** – no Vietnamese necessary.

HANOI HILTON

With gallows humour US prisoners of war dubbed **Hoa Lo Prison** the Hanoi Hilton. Sections inside the forbidding walls were also euphemistically named – Heartbreak Hotel, for example, described the solitary confinement cells measuring 1.8m x 1.8m (6ft x 6ft). Built by the French in the early 20th century, the site, in Hoa Lo Street, has been redeveloped with a complex that includes, ironically, a luxury hotel.

HANOI'S ORIGINS

In AD1010, as legend has it, **Ly Thai To** was seeking the site of a new capital. While cruising the Red River, he saw a dragon preparing to take wing – an auspicious sign. So, on this spot, Ly Thai To built Thang Long – the Soaring Dragon – now Southeast Asia's oldest surviving capital. Over the centuries the name changed, to **Dong Kinh** (from which the Europeans derived their name for northern Vietnam, **Tonkin**), and finally, in 1831, to **Ha Noi** (City by the River).

Left: *The grim exterior of the former 'Hanoi Hilton' prison no longer inspires fear.*

HANOI MUSEUMS

Highly recommended museums (usually closed for two-hour lunches and on Mondays) include:

History Museum, 1 Pho Pham Ngu Lao Street, a beautiful building holding a fine, vast collection of artefacts from all periods of Vietnam's past.

Museum of Ethnography, Van Huyen Street, Hanoi's newest museum, well worth the 7km (4-mile) trek to see a vast collection of artefacts and costumes of the 54 ethnic minorities.

Women's Museum, 36 Pho Ly Thuong Kiet, inevitably patriotic, but also holding a collection of minority traditional costumes.

Ho Chi Minh Museum, Bao Tang Ho Chi Minh, documentation and memorabilia of the country's founding father.

Cai leung is an amalgam of **cheo**, the earliest form of folk mime and spoken drama. Plots, set in feudal days, are often comic to the point of farce with clearly recognizable heroes and villains, irreverently poking fun at feudal officials. One of the most beautiful, poignant and funny, is a dramatization of Vietnam's epic poem, *Kieu*, composed by poet Nguyen Du (1765–1820). The costumes are colourful, the traditional music a delightful challenge to the ear. Get a Vietnamese speaker to ask about performances (72 Hang Bac Street, tel: 4 3825 7823).

BA DINH DISTRICT AND THE WEST LAKE

Immediately west of the Old Town is the huge open space once occupied by the Citadel. This was the site of the **Imperial Palace** of the late **Le dynasty**, mostly destroyed in the 17th century. Later fortifications built on the same site have similarly vanished except for the North Gate on Phan Dinh Phung Street and the hexagonal Flag Tower (Cot Co) on Dien Bien Phu Street, built in 1812 and now a Hanoi landmark.

Further northwest lies the southern shore of **West Lake** (Ho Tay) which at 583ha (1440 acres), is Hanoi's largest lake, separated by a narrow causeway (Thanh Nien Street) from the smaller **White Silk Lake** (Ho Truc Bach). The creation of Ho Tay is credited variously to a stampeding golden buffalo calf or a dragon-king.

LOTUS SYMBOL

Rising above the water on its single column the One Pillar Pagoda represents a lotus flower. The flower is a Buddhist symbol; just as the lotus has its roots buried in mud under water, yet manages to rise above the surface and open its flower in the sunlight, so the Buddha was born in the impure world but through his Enlightenment he rose above it.

Tran Quoc and Quan Thanh Pagodas ★★

One of Hanoi's oldest temples, **Tran Quoc** Pagoda was originally built on the banks of the Red River but moved in the 17th century to its present site beside the causeway on West Lake's southeastern shore. A stele dated 1639 records the temple's history. At the southern end of the causeway, **Quan Thanh** is a typically ornate temple honouring Tran Vo, guardian spirit of the north. Noted for its large bronze bell, cast in 1677, and its towering bronze statue of Tran Vo, the temple originally dates from the 11th or 12th century, during the Le dynasty, although it has subsequently been reconstructed twice.

Above: *Rising out of its lotus pond, the One Pillar Pagoda is one of the delights of Hanoi.*
Opposite: *In a peaceful spot overlooking the West Lake, Tran Quoc's name translates as 'Defence of the Country'.*

One Pillar Pagoda (Chua Mot Cot) ★★★

Elegantly raised on a single column above a pond and designed to represent a lotus emerging from the water, this charming little wooden pagoda is near Ho Chi Minh's Mausoleum. It was originally built in the 11th century by **Emperor Ly Thai To** who, lacking an heir, dreamt he was presented with a male child seated on a lotus flower by **Quan An**, the Goddess of Mercy. A short while later, the emperor married a peasant girl who gave birth to a son and heir. In gratitude Ly Thai To built the **One Pillar Pagoda**. This highly revered shrine has been rebuilt several times, most notably in the fifties after it was torched by the French during their final retreat from Hanoi in 1954. The nearby Bo tree was a gift from India, planted in 1958. In the same compound is the pretty little **Dien Huu Pagoda**.

Temple of Literature (Van Mieu) ★★★

Open daily 08:00–17:00. This is Hanoi's most impressive temple, notable for its **historical** importance, **architectural** interest and, not least, **meditative atmosphere**. Located in an extensive compound south of the Citadel, between Nguyen Thai Hoc and Quoc Tu Giam streets, the **Temple of Literature** was founded in 1070 by Emperor Le Thanh Tong and dedicated to **Confucius**. Six years later it became the national **university** (Quoc Tu Giam), established to teach the children of royalty and the

> **HO CHI MINH'S MAUSOLEUM**
>
> Directly south of the Presidential Palace is the unmistakable grey marble mausoleum where Ho Chi Minh's mortal remains are preserved in a glass casket. The imposing, but stark, building was constructed between 1973 and 1975. Open 08:00–11:00, Tuesday to Thursday, Saturday and Sunday, December to September.

Right: *Roll of honour –*
successful scholars had
to endure over 30 days of
doctoral examinations
before graduating as
mandarins.

TRADITIONAL MUSIC

Vietnam's delightful music
played on **traditional** musical
instruments – the one-stringed
monochord (*dan bau*), the
16-stringed zither (*dan tranh*),
a long-necked, moon-shaped
guitar (*nguyet*), a pear-shaped
lute (*dan ty ba*), drums,
bamboo flutes, and upright
bamboo xylophones – can
often be heard at the **Temple**
of Literature, upstairs at the
Ho Chi Minh Museum, at the
Water Puppet, **Vietnam**
National Tuong Theatre and
Cai Leung Theatres and in
certain restaurants.

aristocracy (mandarins). The long, narrow temple compound, pleasantly planted with banyan and frangipani, is
divided into five walled courtyards and, despite repeated
renovations, the various halls and pavilions remain fine
examples of traditional architecture. The main entrance is
on the south side (Quoc Tu Giam St), and beyond the first
courtyard is Khue Van Cac (Pavilion Dedicated to the
Constellation of Literature). In the next compound is
Thien Quang Tinh (Well of Heavenly Clarity), and flanking this large pool is the temple's most famous sight – 82
stone stelae resting on the backs of stone tortoises,
inscribed with the names and places of birth of successful
candidates in the doctoral examinations held here
between 1442 and 1780. Another gate leads to the **Great**
House of Ceremonies, where a colossal red statue of
Confucius reigns.

Presidential Palace ★

This early 20th-century French colonial building, located
on Hung Vuong Street, was formerly the residence of
the Governor-General of Indo-China and is today used
for state functions. Reputedly, Ho Chi Minh refused to
live here.

SOUTHEAST OF HOAN KIEM LAKE

South of Hoan Kiem Lake is the former French quarter where the landscape changes to one of broad, leafy boulevards and ochre Paris-style villas, the best of which are now occupied by embassies and government offices.

Opera House ★★★

At the east end of Trang Tien Street, this grand building, completely renovated in 1997, stands as a golden jewel of French colonial culture. A replica of the magnificent Paris Opera built in 1911, it is now less romantically known as the Municipal Theatre. See local newspapers for current performances.

St Joseph's Cathedral (Nha Tho Lon) ★

Situated on Ly Quoc Su Street, the cathedral was con-secrated in 1886. With its twin-tower, neo-Gothic façade and stained-glass windows, it is a startling reminder of European influence. Masses are held daily from 05:00 to 07:00 and from 17:00 to 19:00. At other times the doors may be locked. Visitors should enquire at the nearby Diocese of Hanoi on Nha Chung Street.

Ba Da Pagoda ★

In the street in front of St Joseph's, Nha Tho, is **Ba Da Pagoda** (Heavenly Mistress of the Stone), a Buddhist temple dating from the 15th century. It is easily over-

Left: *The elegant renovated exterior of the French Opera House, now rather unromantically called the Municipal Theatre.*

looked because of its uninspiring exterior, but the interior is surprisingly interesting for its clutter of religious objects and gilt statues of Buddha.

The temple derives its name from a stone statue reputed to have magical properties. The original has since been lost and a wooden replica stands in its place.

Chua Quan Su (Ambassadors' Pagoda) ★★

Southwest of Hoan Kiem, on Quan Su Street, this temple was completed in 1942. It is notable for occupying the site of a 17th-century reception house for visiting **Buddhist** ambassadors and envoys from other Buddhist countries.

DAY EXCURSIONS FROM HANOI
Chua Huong Tich (Fragrant Perfume Pagoda) ★★★

The site of an annual Buddhist pilgrimage (during March and April), this is a series of shrines set in grottoes in the limestone cliffs of Huong Tich Son (Mountain of the Fragrant Traces), 70km (43 miles) southwest of Hanoi. Dating mostly from the 17th century, the pagoda grottoes have evocative names: among others, **Pagoda Leading to Heaven** (Thiem Chua) and **Purgatory Pagoda** (Giai Oan Chua). The site is approached by road, then enchantingly by boat poled along the Yen River. The landscape of limestone mountains and

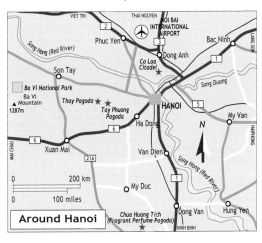

Around Hanoi

green paddy fields makes this one of the most stunning rural scenes in the whole of North Vietnam. (*See* Tam Coc and Hoa Lu, Chapter 3.)

Co Loa ★

The site of Vietnam's very first capital is located in rural Dong Anh district, 15km (9 miles) northwest of Hanoi. Little remains of the once extensive snail-shaped ramparts of the fortified Citadel founded in 255BC, although modern excavations reveal sufficient examples. A temple is dedicated to Emperor An Duong who was defeated by the Chinese when his daughter, married to the son of a Chinese general, revealed the secret of her father's magic crossbow to her husband, thus beginning a thousand years of Chinese domination. A traditional communal house (*dinh*) and a small museum add to the interest. Not monumental, but enough for history enthusiasts.

Above: *Goods on their way to market in time-honoured tradition.*

Thay and Tay Phuong Pagodas ★★★

Both these pagodas, situated some 40km (25 miles) south-west of Hanoi in Ha Son Binh Province, are well worth visiting for their intrinsic interest and lovely settings.

Located at Sai Son Village, **Thay Pagoda** (Pagoda of the Master), officially named Thien Phuc (Heavenly Blessing), dates from the 12th century and is dedicated to Emperor Le Than Tong and Tu Dao Hanh, a monk renowned as an herbalist and a water puppeteer – hence the epithet 'master'. In addition to the temple, the site is notable for its traditional water puppet theatre and the Sai Son hill, whose caves can be explored.

On the seventh day of the third lunar month, the Thay Pagoda Festival provides an excellent opportunity for visitors to watch traditional water puppet theatre in a village setting on the artificial lake said to have been created by Tu Dao Hanh.

Nearby is the hilltop **Tay Phuong Pagoda** (West Pagoda), reached by a flight of some 250 steps. Designed as three buildings with most distinctive roofs, the originally 8th-century pagoda houses many excellent examples of traditional Vietnamese wood sculpture.

HANDICRAFT VILLAGES

In addition to the craft guilds of the Old Town, numerous craft villages supplied the royal court at the Citadel. **Bat Trang**, 13km (8 miles) southeast, is still producing fine ceramics; **Van Phuc**, 8km (5 miles) southwest, is still weaving silk for domestic and export markets; **So**, 25km (15 miles) southeast, is noted for its noodles and **Dong Ky**, 15km (9 miles) northeast, has diversified from producing firecrackers – now banned – to producing inlaid mother-of-pearl furniture.

Hanoi at a Glance

Autumn (**Oct–Nov**) or spring (**Apr–Jul**) are best when the weather is cool and sunny.

Hanoi's sleek **Noi Bai International Airport** is 35km (22 miles) from the city – the journey takes about 1hr. In **Hanoi** you can choose between the slightly more expensive metered airport **taxis**, ordinary metered city taxis and a cheap, convenient airport mini-bus which, for a small extra cost, will drop you at your hotel. International **trains** run from Hanoi to Nanning and Kunming.

Taxis cruise the streets and can be booked by phone or found near hotels. **Taxi** operators include: Mai Linh Taxi, tel: 4 3822 2666, 4 3822 2555; ABC Taxi, tel: 4 3719 1919; Noi Bai Taxi, tel: 4 3886 8888, www.noibaitaxi.com (cheapest from the airport, book in advance). Self-drive **hire cars** are not available. Hiring a **car and driver** at a daily rate is relatively inexpensive for longer journeys. Tourist cafés offer cheap **day trips** to many tourist sites including **Ha Long Bay**. Short distances in town are most easily covered by taxi, *cyclo* (pedicabs) or *xe oms* (motorbike taxis). Hanoi's public buses are impractical for the visitor. Sightseeing is best done **walking** or, for the intrepid in view of Hanoi's traffic, by **bicycle**. Bikes can be rented.

Hanoi now boasts numerous hotels of international standard, and the quality of accommodation has risen dramatically in the past few years.

LUXURY
Sofitel Metropole Hanoi, 15 Ngo Quyen Street, tel: 4 3826 6919, www.sofitel.com
Hilton Hanoi Opera, 1 Le Thanh Tong Street, tel: 4 3933 0500; fax: 4 3933 0530, hanoi @hilton.com Huge monument to modernity, opened in 1999.
Melia Hanoi, 44 Ly Thuong Kiet Street, tel: 4 3934 3343, www.meliahanoi.com Even more sumptuous, built on the site of the prison.

MID-RANGE
Zephyr Hotel, 4-6 Ba Trieu Str, tel: 4 3934 1256, fax: 4 3934 1262, zephyrhotel@ vnn.vn www.zephyrhotel. com.vn Elegant hotel beside Hoan Kiem Lake. Free gym, fruit and breakfast.
Hoa Binh Hotel, 27 Ly Thuong Kiet, tel: 4 3825 3315, fax: 4 3826 9818, kshoabinh@ hn.vnn.vn http://hoabinh hotel.com Luxurious French colonial splendour south of Hoan Kiem Lake.
Hong Ngoc Hotel, 30-34 Hang Manh St, tel: 4 3828 5053, fax: 4 3827 5054, hotline: 4 904 428 387, reservation@hong ngochotels.com www.hong ngochotel.com Luxury at medium rates; restaurant, sauna, cable TV (English), central.

Lucky Hotel, 11 Ngo Huyen, tel: 4 3928 7989, fax: 4 9287 893, hanoiluckyhotel@ gmail.com www.hanoilucky hotel.com Near Hoan Kiem Lake. Free Internet, TV.

BUDGET
Classic Hotel II, 49 Luong Ngoc Quyen St, tel: 4 3926 1106, www.classichotel hanoi.com A comfortable mini-hotel in the Old Town north of Hoan Kiam Lake.
Hanoi Legend Hotel, 47 Luong Ngoc Quyen Str, tel: 4 3926 2749, fax: 4 3826 8459, hanoilegendhotel@live.com www.hanoilegendhotel.com Family mini-hotel, large rooms, tub/showers, cable TV, in the old town.
Nam Phuong Hotel, 16 Bao Khanh Str, tel: 4 3928 5085, fax: 4 3825 8964, kts.hotels andtravel@gmail.com Clean, cheap, cheerful and central.

LUXURY
Club Opera, 59 Ly Thai To Street, tel: 4 3824 6950. Cosy, chic atmosphere across from the Sofitel, mid-price.
Nineteen 11, 01 Trang Tien Str, tel: 4 3933 4801, www.nineteen11.com.vn Exquisite food, inventive Belgian chef, tasteful decor.
Bleu de Thuy, 28 Tong Duy Tan, tel: 4 3928 5900. French and Vietnamese food.
Green Mango, 18 Hang Quat Street, tel: 4 3928 3316, www.greenmango.vn Smooth French-Vietnamese-

owned restaurant. Serves excellent food.

Le Tonkin, 14 Ngo Van So, tel: 4 3943 3457. Tropical garden, elegant villa, serves exquisitely presented Vietnamese food.

Indochine, 16 Pham Ngu Lao St, tel: 4 3942 4097. A vast Vietnamese menu, try prawns steamed in a coconut shell.

Hoa Sua, 28A Ha Hoi Str, tel: 4 3942 4448. Dine on the terrace of this villa and try the French or Vietnamese food to help the street children, who train here as chefs and waiters.

Mediterraneo, 23 Nha Tho Street, tel: 4 3826 6288. Home-made pasta, Italian chef, great for street watching.

Hanoi is good for silk – try 'Silk Street', **Hang Gai** – in the old town. Other good buys are gold jewellery, jade, amber, lacquer, ceramics, embroidered **T-shirts**, **brocade**, **sculpture**, **paintings** and **antiques** (check if export is permitted; customs confiscate items on departure). For paintings, check the galleries along **Pho Trang Tien**, **Hang Gai** and, its extension, **Hang Bong Street.** For Vietnam's top **artists**, contact Suzanne Lecht's gallery, **Art Vietnam**, 7 Nguyen Khac Nhu, tel: 4 3927 2349, info@artvietnamgallery.com

http://artvietnamgallery.com who arranges exhibitions abroad. For **jewellery**, compare the shops along **Hang Bac Street**. For books about Vietnam in English, French and Vietnamese, contact **The Gioi Publishers** at 46 Tran Hung Dao Street, tel: 4 3825 3841, fax: 4 3826 9567, thegioi@hn.vnn.vn www.thegioipublishers.com.vn

Exotissimo Travel, 26 Tran Nhat Duat St, tel: 4 3827 2150, tnd@exotissimo.com www.exotissimo.com No groups, tailor-made only.

Handspan Adventure Travel, 70-80 Ma May, tel: 4 3926 2828, fax: 4 3926 2383, info@handspan.com www.handspan.com

Kangaroo Café, 18 Bao Khanh Street, tel: 4 3827 9931, kangaroo@kangaroocafe.com www.kangaroocafe.com The only expat-operated travel café in Hanoi.

Vietnamopentour-Sinhcafe,

66 Hang Than, tel: 4 3836 4212, sinhcafetour@hn.vnn.vn www.sinhcafe.com

International Hospital, 1 Phuong Mai Street, Dong Da District, tel: 4 3577 1100, emergencies: 4 3574 1111, fax: 4 3576 4443, www.hfh.com.vn

Hanoi Family Medical Practice, Van Phuc Compound, 298 I Kim Ma Road, Ba Dinh District, Hanoi, tel: 4 3843 3843, hanoi@vietnammedical practice.com www.vietnam medicalpractice.com

Pediatric Clinic, 298 D Kim Ma Road, tel: 4 3843 0748.

Viet Duc Hospital, 40 Trang Tri Street, tel: 4 3825 3531, fax: 4 3824 8308, bvvd@fpt.vn www.vietduchospital.edu.vn

International SOS, 1 Dang Thai Mai, tel: 4 3934 0666, www.internationalsos.com

Vietnam Airlines, 53 Quang Trung, tel: 4 3832 0320, www.vietnamair.com.vn

Air Asia, www.airasia.com Budget airline flying from Bangkok to Hanoi and Ho Chi Minh City.

Jetstar, www.jetstar.com Budget airline flying from many Asian destinations and within Vietnam.

HANOI	J	F	M	A	M	J	J	A	S	O	N	D
AVERAGE TEMP. °F	61	62	68	74	81	83	84	82	80	76	70	64
AVERAGE TEMP. °C	16	17	20	23	27	29	29	28	27	25	21	18
RAINFALL in	1	1	2	3	8	10	13	14	10	4	2	1
RAINFALL mm	18	26	44	90	188	240	288	318	265	130	43	24
DAYS OF RAINFALL	8	11	15	13	14	15	16	17	14	9	7	6

3
The North

It is easy to think of Hanoi as being at the very top of Vietnam, although in fact a considerable expanse of territory stretches north and west from the capital to the Chinese and Laotian borders. This highland region is Vietnam's historic heartland, the land fought over by the early Viets and the Chinese. It is attractive for its extraordinary mountainous landscapes (some of the finest in the country) and its rich assortment of hill tribe minorities, including the Dao, H'mong, Coin, Man, Lu, Tay, Nung, Black and White T'ai, and Muong, each with its distinctive sartorial style.

The North, as referred to by the Vietnamese, extends southwards from the Chinese border to just above the city of Hue – the 17th parallel was the former division between North and South Vietnam. In outline, the region is shaped like a club, the rounded 'head' at the top comprising mountains and the delta plains of the **Red River**, the 'handle' at the bottom formed by a narrow coastal plain backed by the northern span of the **Truong Son** mountain range.

However, it should be remembered that the area has only recently been added to the travel map, and tourism facilities in some areas are comparatively sparse.

Apart from short day trips, essentially there are three recommended excursion options from Hanoi: a journey east to Ha Long Bay and Cat Ba Island National Park; a journey north to Sa Pa to visit the minority *montagnard* tribes and a journey northeast to visit Ba Be Lakes as well as hill tribes.

DON'T MISS

*** Ha Long Bay: behold a haunting seascape.
** Cat Ba National Park: view a rich variety of flora, fauna and good beaches.
** Sa Pa: see spectacular mountain scenery and minority hill people.
** Ba Be Lakes: witness more stunning scenery and minority hill tribes.
** Hoa Lu and Tam Coc: visit the temples of Vietnam's first recorded capital and float through stunning 'Halong of the rice plains'.

Opposite: *A typical northern landscape in lush Hoa Binh Province.*

The most convenient way to make an excursion into the mountainous north is by hiring a car or four-wheel-drive **vehicle** and a **driver** in Hanoi. However, Hanoi travel agencies and tourist cafés have made it easy with a wide variety of tours, some for adventurous trekkers, others for sedentary observers. Roads to the main centres have improved, but remain poor – or non-existent – in remote areas. Alternatively, there are **rail** links between **Hanoi** and **Lao Cai** (12hr), which is the nearest rail point for **Sa Pa**, and northeast to **Lang Son** (6hr) on the Chinese border, from which there are buses.

EAST OF HANOI
Ha Long Bay ★★★

Spectacular **Ha Long Bay** with its mysterious limestone karsts erupting abruptly from the jade green sea has quite justifiably been named a World Heritage Site by UNESCO. At any time of year, even during the mists of winter, this landscape is beguiling, constantly changing as your boat edges closer, weaving amongst the labyrinth of this colossal green maze.

Ha Long Bay is an archipelago of some 3000 islands, both huge and miniscule, belonging to the coastal province of **Quang Ninh** and covering about 1500km² (579 sq miles).

The name Ha Long translates to 'where the dragon descends into the sea'. A local legend relates how this seascape was created when a giant dragon dashed down from the mountains to the coast, its footprints gouging the upturned karsts as it plunged into the sea. A number of caves and grottoes, some illuminated, can be visited, the finest being the huge Hang Dau Go Cave which, with its superb stalactites and stalagmites, was appropriately named *Grotte des Merveilles* (Grotto of Wonders) by the French. Some caves have yielded artefacts confirming that humanity has inhabited these regions for 6000 years.

Ha Long City, 160km (101 miles) east of Hanoi on a splendid new motorway, lies divided by the bay, with **Bai Chay** on the south bank and **Hon Gai** on the north. Most

Opposite Top: *Ha Long Bay has some spectacular caves and grottoes, many of which can be visited by boat from Haiphong and Hon Gai.*
Opposite Bottom: *In the Red River Delta the prime money-earner is rice.*
Right: *Ha Long Bay, a watery green maze that seems to go on forever.*

hotels and restaurants are in Bai Chay. Although Bai Chay lies on a long, wide beach, it is muddy and not particularly appealing. Also, in recent years Ha Long City has turned itself into a 'pleasure centre' for Hanoians and even the Chinese, who come south seeking 'Thai massage' – a euphemism for prostitution. Particularly in the popular summer months, there is no real reason to stay in Ha Long Bay other than to catch a boat for a tour through the islands. The easy option is to book a tour from Hanoi that includes the bus, hotel, meals and sometimes a night aboard a comfortable boat en route to **Cat Ba Island**.

Haiphong

Located on the right bank of the **Cam River** and supporting a population of 1.8 million in the greater metropolitan area, Haiphong was largely created by the French in the late 19th century. What had been just a small harbour was then transformed into a busy commercial centre and port designed to rival Hong Kong.

Historically, the city is best known for a tragic

DIEN BIEN PHU

In 1954, towards the end of the First Indo-China War, the French set up a garrison at **Dien Bien Phu**. The plan was to cut off Viet Minh access to Laos, but instead the French became trapped when the Viet Minh unexpectedly reinforced the surrounding hills and masterminded a siege. Finally, after assaults and bombard-ments, lasting 57 days, the French were forced to surrender. Although the Vietnamese suffered heavy casualties, their victory at Dien Bien Phu virtually won them the war.

BACH DANG

Some 10km (6 miles) east of Haiphong, the Bach Dang River (also known variously as the Cam River or the Haiphong Channel) meets the sea in a complex of channels. It is a historic spot where the Vietnamese repeatedly repulsed Chinese invasion attempts. A most famous event was in 1289, when Tran Hung Dao planted spikes in the water and so destroyed the ships of the Mongol fleet.

incident that sparked the First **Indo-China War**. In 1946, when tension was running high between France and Vietnam, the French bombarded **Haiphong** and inflicted huge casualties on the civilian population. A few weeks later war broke out. The city suffered further bombing during the Second Indo-China War. In the last few years there has been much rebuilding and new industrial expansion.

Although **Haiphong** has been ravaged by latter-day development, a certain amount of colonial architecture survives, and ports tend to have a fascination of their own. For most visitors a half-day's sightseeing is sufficient. Among the city's most ornate buildings, the 300-year-old **Du Hang Pagoda** is a notable example of traditional Vietnamese architecture, and the Hang Kenh Communal House, (once a community centre and temple), has a remarkable collection of 500 wood carvings.

Situated halfway up **Elephant Mount**, on a rocky hill on the outskirts of Haiphong, the **Chi Lai Communal House** has been converted into a museum displaying Neolithic bronzes. The caves on the mount were used as a guerrilla base during the war with the French. In the war with the USA, there was an anti-aircraft battery where female gunners reputedly downed US fighter planes. Alternatively, should you find yourself in Haiphong with an afternoon between flight and hydrofoil, visit Do Son beach resort (first developed by the French and still popular with Hanoians and expats), located on a long hilly promontory some 20km (12 miles) southeast of Haiphong. The 4km (2.5 miles) long promontory ends in a string of islets. Apart from the beach, Do Son is also the site of the first casino in Vietnam (established in 1975). It is open to foreigners only.

Cat Ba Island **

Lying about 30km (19 miles) from Ha Long City, a fast (45-minute), or slow (4-hour), boat ride away, this large inhabited island covers an area of 354km² (137 sq miles). About half of it is protected as a national park. Characterized by spectacular 300m (985ft) limestone cliffs, the island was once a pirate haunt but is now noted for its surprising range of **natural habitats** – tropical evergreen forest, freshwater lake, mangrove, sandy shore and coral reef – supporting a rich variety of

Opposite: *Characteristic minority architecture near Sa Pa. At high altitudes, where there is little risk of flooding, homes do not need to be raised on stilts.*

The North

KIEP BAC PAGODA

Tran Hung Dao is revered as a kind of guardian spirit. A temple in his honour, dating from the 13th century, is located 61km (38 miles) from Hanoi, 15km (9 miles) north of Hai Dong, en route to Ha Long Bay. A popular annual festival is held at the temple on the anniversary of his death on the 20th of the 8th lunar month (September/October).

MINORITIES

Minority peoples inhabiting
the northern highlands include
the **T'ai** (with Black, Red and
White subgroups), **Nung,
Muong, Giay, H'mong** (Meo)
and **Dao**. Some, like the T'ai
and Muong, are traditionally
valley dwellers who were
forced into the hills by successive invasions long ago.
Others, like the H'mong, Dao
and Nung, are descendants of
ancient migrants who settled
in the high border areas.
Seminomadic in lifestyle, each
group has a distinct culture and
is most readily identified by the
traditional dress of the women.

wildlife, including monkeys, deer, gibbons, wild boar and
hornbills. The island offers an attractive mix of forested
hills, waterfalls and caves, as well as beaches and a busy
waterfront scene in **Cat Ba Town**.

NORTH OF HANOI
Sa Pa ★★

Those with more time might take a bus or a (12-hour) train
to Lao Cai, the border town and railhead for **Sa Pa**, now
fully reconstructed after being destroyed by the Chinese in
1979. There are daily markets but the big market in Sa Pa
is on Sunday where **Black H'mong** and **Red Dao** push
their wares rather aggressively.

Although Vietnam's highest mountain peak, **Fansipan**,
standing at 3143m (10,215ft), can be seen from Sa Pa
on a clear day, it can only be reached on foot and the
trip with a guide takes at least three days. There are no
huts or facilities; self-sufficient camping gear and food
must be carried.

From Sa Pa, a four-wheel-drive vehicle is necessary to
get to **Bac Ha** (Sunday market) to see **Flower H'mong** and
Dao minorities, or from Bac Ha to Can Cau (Saturday
market) in the mountains of the Flower H'mong people. A
much smaller market in the mountains at **Can Cau** can be
reached over a bumpy road, slowly, with a normal car.

A northwest loop from Sa Pa might include the two
markets at **Binh Lu** and **Cam Duong** (Flowering H'mong,
Dao, Tien, Coin, Man and Lu) then on to Lai Chau,
passing through remote, forested highlands of stunning
beauty, then south to the battlefield of Dien Bien Phu near
the Laos border, where the French were decisively defeated
by the **Viet Minh** in 1954. A small museum, along with a
reconstruction of the French command post and a few
other reminders of the battle, can be seen at the site. There
are separate monuments honouring the Viet Minh and the
French who died. The attractive valley and surrounding
mountains evoke a tingling sensation of remoteness, while
scattered in the hills are villages of Thai and other minority
groups. At **Cam Duong** overnight home-stays can be
arranged (a permit is required) with minority peoples.

Left: *Valley-dwelling minorities eke out a living by farming and rearing livestock such as chickens, ducks and pigs.*

Ba Be Lake ★★

From Hanoi, a northeast loop aiming for Ba Be Lake – actually three lakes linked together, fed by the Nang River – would pause at the town of Thai Nguyen to visit the **Museum of Ethnography**, pass through Bac Can and arrive at Ba Be Lake in the evening. After sleeping in the village of **Cho Ra** on the lake shore, a boat takes you to visit Puong Cave en route to Pac Ngoi village (Tay and Nung people) on the far side of the lake. This is followed by a walk to **Dau Dang Waterfall** which offers breathtaking scenery and the opportunity to visit hill people at **Pac Ngoi** village before returning to **Bac Can**. From here one would travel north to **Cao Bang** near the Chinese border to see **Ban Doc Waterfall** and then south again via Lang Son (Nhi Thanh and Tam Thanh caves), to Hanoi.

SOUTH OF HANOI

Mai Chau

En route to Sa Pa, Mai Chau, 135km (73 miles) southwest of Hanoi is the nearest place to see minority people in a sprinkling of rural hamlets on a day excursion from Hanoi. Overnight stays in a **White Thai** stilt house can be arranged, also treks to a Lac village (Ban Lac) and a H'mong village (Xa Linh).

Hoa Lu and Tam Coc ★★

Attractively sited in a mountain setting at the village of **Truong Yen**, 102km (65 miles) south of Hanoi, **Hoa Lu**

CUC PHUONG NATIONAL PARK

Located west of Nam Dinh, 140km (87 miles) from Hanoi, Cuc Phuong is one of Vietnam's few national parks, established in 1962. An area of primary tropical forest, the preserve extends over 25,000ha (61,728 acres) and shelters an immensely varied list of flora (nearly 2000 species) and fauna (animals, 64 species; reptiles, 33; birds, 137). Caves in the limestone mountains have yielded prehistoric finds.

HIGHWAY 1

One of the longest and most famous roads in Southeast Asia is Highway 1. It links Hanoi with Ho Chi Minh City, although its full length runs from Lang Son, near the Chinese border in the north, to Tay Ninh, near the border with Cambodia in the south. In all it covers a distance of some 2000km (1250 miles). In recent years this main artery has been improved with the exception of certain stretches, mostly in the south, where it is little better than a two-lane rural road.

was an Imperial City during the pre-Hanoi Dinh (968–80) and Early Le (980–1009) dynasties. The entire former capital lies destroyed beneath the rice paddies, although archaeological investigation has revealed much of historical and artistic interest. The only sites remaining of the Citadel are two temples, **Dinh Tien Hoang**, temple of the Dinh emperors, and **Dai Hanh**, temple of the Early Le emperors.

Known as 'Ha Long Bay of the rice paddies', a watery plain, from which huge limestone karsts rear up abruptly resembling those in Guilin and Yangshuo in China, is located at nearby Tam Coc. Geographically it is the extension of adjacent land that did not sink beneath the waves covered by Ha Long Bay. The delightful means of visiting the caves – Tam Coc means 'three caves' – is by rowboat along the Ngo Dong River in which ducks dive and young boys fish with baskets. The caves are more like tunnels than caves; the first measures 127m (413ft) long, the second 70m (228ft) and the third 40m (130ft) long. The boats float through them, the boat girls paddling nimbly with one foot. At the end is a small lake where invariably there is a boat-jam of floating vendors keen on selling soft drinks and embroidery from nearby Van Lan village to a captive clientele. Hanoi 'tourist cafés' organize combined day trips to Hoa Lu and Tam Coc.

Phat Diem

Most visitors fly from Hanoi to Hue, taking day trips to tourist sites north, east and south of the capital. For dedicated overlanders, 30km (19 miles) southeast of Ninh Binh, Phat Diem is the site of a noted 19th-century Catholic **cathedral**, an eccentric oriental structure built in Sino-Vietnamese style.

Vinh and Kim Lien Village

Located some 291km (182 miles) south of Hanoi, Vinh is notable only as an overnight stop on the overland journey from Hanoi to Hue.

Kim Lien Village, some 14km (9 miles) northwest of Vinh, is famous as the birthplace of Ho Chi Minh. There

VIRGIN CAVE

One of the grottoes in Ha Long Bay is named Virgin Cave and, like many famous sites in Vietnam, it honours local womanhood. An old folk tale records how a young fishergirl was demanded by a rich man in payment of a debt owed to him by her parents. She refused to submit to the man and was imprisoned in the cave where she died of starvation.

are in fact two separate family compounds; the mother's home, where Ho was born, and his father's house, where he spent his early youth. There is also a small **museum** (mainly a photographic record of Ho) in this quiet, well-tended and curiously emotive spot.

Annam Gate (Ngang Pass)

Continuing south overland, lying on the 18th parallel, a small range of mountains forms the historical divide between the land of the Viets and the Kingdom of Champa. In colonial times, the mountains marked the division between the French provinces of Tonkin and Annam. Reaching up to a height of 1000m (3300ft), the mountains close in on Highway 1 and the road briefly joins the coast.

17th Parallel

A little way south of the town of Dong Hoi, lies the 17th Parallel that once divided North and South Vietnam. The border is physically marked by Hien Luong Bridge, carrying Highway 1 over the Ben Hai River. Prior to 1967, the northern half of the bridge was painted red and the southern half yellow. Dong Ha, the capital of Quang Tri Province, is some 72km (45 miles) north of Hue.

> **THE DMZ**
>
> The Demilitarized Zone (DMZ) was established during the Vietnam War as a buffer zone. It extended 5km (3 miles) on either side of the border that separated North from South Vietnam. On the southern side of the DMZ, west of Dong Ha, there were several US firebases, but now much of the area has been developed as rubber planta-tions. Although most visible signs of the war have vanished, unexploded mines and artillery shells still present hidden dan-gers, which tragically continue to cause injury and death.

Left: *These northern children find natural shelter from a passing cloudburst.*

The North at a Glance

For Ha Long Bay, the best months are from **Feb–Jul**, but don't be put off between **November** and **April** when it is mild and misty, just expect occasional rain. For the mountains, the best months are from **Apr–Jun** and **Aug–Oct**. **Apr–Sep** is hot and humid, with heavy rain. The coldest months, November to April, are grey, wet, muddy and the nights bitterly cold.

To Ha Long Bay from Hanoi, there are regular **train** (3 hours) and **minibus** (3.5 hours) connections. To Haiphong there are less frequent train (2 hours) and minibus (2 hours) con-nections. There are **boats** and **ferries** linking Ha Long Bay and Cat Ba Island, plus **hydrofoil** services between Haiphong and Cat Ba. For a quick visit, **Vietnam Airlines** flies from Ho Chi Minh City and Da Nang to Haiphong, from which there are slow (2.5 hours) and fast (1 hour) boats and hydrofoils to Cat Ba Island. The mountainous north is accessible by **car with driver** or by train or bus through tours offered by Hanoi travel agencies and tourist cafés. There is a good (overnight) train service in a soft sleeper to Lao Cai, the nearest rail point to Sa Pa. Alternatively, Vietnam Airlines operates flights to Dien Bien Phu from Hanoi (1 hour).

In **Ha Long Bay** distances are sometimes long and uphill. There are inexpensive metered taxis and motorbike taxis (*xe om*) – no **cyclos**. In the highlands, **cars** and **four-wheel-drive vehicles** can be rented at a daily rate from main hotels and travel agents. Getting to remote tribes involves trekking; the less energetic can encounter tribal people in local markets.

Ha Long
The standard of hotels is good here, but the best solution is to book a two- or three-day tour, through a tourist café in Hanoi. These include the bus, sometimes a night in Ha Long Bay and a boat excursion (some with a night spent on board and a night in Cat Ba).

LUXURY
Halong Plaza, 8 Ha Long Road, tel: 33 3845 810, info@halongplaza.com www.halongplaza.com Top of the range, facing the bay.
Heritage, 88 Ha Long Road, tel: 33 3846 888, heritage reservation@gmail.com www.heritagehalonghotel. com A bay-facing, centrally located luxury hotel.
Grand Halong Hotel, Halong Street, tel: 33 3844 041, grandhalong@vnn.vn www.grandhalonghotel. com.vn New centrally located hotel overlooking the bay. Has a pool.

MID-RANGE
Mithrin Hotel, Hoang Quoc Viet Rd, Bai Chay, tel: 33 384 8090, fax: 33 384 1770, gm@ mithrinhotelhalong.com.vn www.mithrinhotelhalong. com.vn Luxury at half the price, spectacular bay views.
Halong Spring Hotel, Halong Road, tel: 33 384 6381, suoimohotel@hn.vnn.vn www.suoimohotel.com New hotel with pool and bay views, near the centre.
Saigon Halong Hotel, Halong Road, tel: 33 384 5845, sahahotel@hn.vnn.vn www.saigonhalonghotel.com Huge, comfy bay-view rooms, centrally located.

BUDGET
Sunlight, 88 Hung Thang, tel: 33 384 8379, sunlighthotel@ hn.vnn.vn www.sunlighthotel halong.com.vn Charming hotel, best bargain bay views.
Cong Doan Halong Hotel, Halong Street, tel: 33 384 6780, congdoanhotel@ hn.vnn.vn Excellent value, central location.
BMC Thang Long Hotel, Halong Road, tel: 33 384 5985, nga.dang.thu@gmail. com www.bmc-thanglong-hotel.com Very pleasant hotel, near the port, good bay views.

Haiphong
LUXURY
Harbour View Hotel, 4 Tran Phu Street, tel: 33 382 7827, info@harbourviewvietnam.com www.harbourviewvietnam.com Elegant French colonial style.

MID-RANGE

Huu Nghi Hotel, 60 Dien Bien Phu, tel: 31 382 1361, huunghi hotel@hn.vnn.vn www.huu nghihotel.vn Central, pleasant.

BUDGET

Khach San Thang Nam, 57 Dien Bien Phu, tel: 31 382 3244, lidanauungai@gmail. com Central, Indochine style, good value.

Cat Ba Island

Development has exploded and new hotels have sprung up along the bay promenade with a luxury resort around the headland. For convenience, stay in town as there are no taxis, only motorbike taxis (*xe on*), although with reservations, resort and hotel minibuses meet arrivals at the port. Despite the peculiar addresses, all these hotels line the bay in Cat Ba town except the Cat Ba Resort-Sunrise Hotel.

LUXURY

Cat Ba Resort-Sunrise Hotel, Cat Co 3 Beach, tel: 31 388 7360, info@catbasunriseresort. com www.catbasunrise resort.com New rustic style hotel with pool out of town, overlooking the beach.

MID-RANGE

Holiday View Hotel, Road 1/4, tel: 31 388 7200, sales@ holidayviewhotel.catba.com www.holidayviewhotel-catba.com Sleek new high-rise, bay-facing hotel at the quiet, beach end of town.

Sunflower Hotel, Nui Ngoc Rd, tel: 31 388 8429 or 388 8890, sunflowerhotel@hn. vnn.vn www.sunflowerhotels. com.vn Pleasant, good standard high-rise with lift a few steps from the bay promenade.

Princes Hotel, Nui Ngoc Road, tel: 31 388 8892 and 31 388 8899, princeshotel@hn.vnn.vn www.catbaprinceshotel.com Agreeable hotel with lift, half a block from the bay.

BUDGET

Bay View Hotel, T6 20 – Khu 4, tel: 31 368 8241, mobile: 0904 522 428. Huge rooms, great value, new Brit-owned mini-hotel on the promenade.

Hoang Ngoc Hotel, 1-4 Street, 20 Group, Area 4, tel: 313 688 788, fax: 313 688 555. New mini-hotel, quiet, comfortable rooms facing the bay.

Ha Long Bay

Several restaurants along the waterfront in Ha Long Bay serve tasty seafood dishes. Look for a crowd of locals and expats.

Cat Ba Island

Green Mango, Group 19, Block 4, tel: 313 887 151, catba@greenmango.vn Sister restaurant to the one in Hanoi, excellent Vietnamese and fusion cuisine.

Noble House Hotel/ Restaurant and SloPony (rock climbing/adventure tours), 4 1/4 Street, tel: 313 368 8450, info@slopony.com www.slo pony.com Cheap rooms, best pizza in Cat Ba; only American tour operator in Vietnam.

To eliminate the hassle of independent touring, it is highly recommended that you book a tour through a Hanoi travel agent or tourist café to Ha Long Bay, Cat Ba or the Highlands. *See* page 45 for travel agents.

LUXURY TOURS

Victoria Sapa Hotel, tel: 20 387 1522, resa.sapa@victoria hotels-asia.com www.victoria hotels-asia.com Arranges a train and hotel package in private rail carriages to Sa Pa.

Kangaroo Café, 18 Bao Kanh Street, Hanoi, tel: 4 3828 9931, kangaroo@kangaroocafe.com www.kangaroocafe.com Small groups and comfortable boats on Halong Bay to Cat Ba Island.

THE NORTH	J	F	M	A	M	J	J	A	S	O	N	D
AVERAGE TEMP. °F	61	61	66	74	81	82	84	82	81	77	70	64
AVERAGE TEMP. °C	16	16	19	23	27	28	29	28	27	25	21	18
RAINFALL in	1	1	2	3	9	11	15	18	12	5	1	1
RAINFALL mm	21	28	43	78	225	291	372	459	315	127	38	19
DAYS OF RAINFALL	6	9	12	10	12	14	16	17	14	8	5	5

4
Central Vietnam: Hue to Hoi An

The slender waist of **Central Vietnam** separates the flood plains of the Red River in the north from the rice bowl of the Mekong Delta to the south. The region is not only physically different due to its rugged **Truong Son Mountains** brooding over the coastal strip, it also has a distinct history, both ancient and modern.

From the 2nd to the 15th centuries AD, the region was dominated by the **Chams**, whose kingdom experienced mixed fortunes in struggles, first against the Khmer to the west, and later against the Vietnamese, who exerted pressure from the north.

Gradually wrested from the Chams by the Vietnamese, relentlessly pushing their borders south, Central Vietnam reached the peak of political importance in the early 19th century when **Hue**, the region's major city, became the capital during the **Nguyen dynasty**. Yet even when first-city status reverted to Hanoi under the French, and Ho Chi Minh City became a power base in the south, Hue remained aloof, as the epitome of cultural refinement, style and conservatism.

Laid out below the dense green of the Truong Son Mountains and straddling the placid **Perfume River** (Song Huong), despite suffering cruelly during three successive wars (1943–75), the city remains enchanting with its haunting **Citadel**, lavish **imperial tombs** and lovely **pagodas**, all of which impart a profound sense of Vietnam's recent imperial past.

Travelling south, Highway 1 cuts through beautiful land and seascapes, lush green paddies in a kaleidoscope of

DON'T MISS

*** Hue's Citadel: the former Imperial City, Hue.
*** Hue: pleasure gardens and temple tombs of the Nguyen emperors.
*** Museum of Cham Sculpture: a fine collection of 7th- to 15th-century carving, Da Nang.
*** Historic houses: Hoi An, an ancient port town in a time capsule.
** My Son: a vast complex of sacred Cham towers and temples.

Opposite: *Breathtaking views of sea and sky from Hai Van Pass, between Hue and Da Nang.*

greens hemmed in by mountains and seas. The road slowly climbs 1219m (4000ft) to **Hai Van Pass**, which the French called *Col des Nuages* (Hill of the Clouds), and where, if it's clear, the view of the paddies and beaches below is spectacular. The road glides down past an idyllic lagoon and fishing village, **Lan Co** (where big plans for hotels were arrested by recession in Japan) to **Da Nang**, Vietnam's fourth largest city and major port.

Da Nang has played a major role in Vietnam's history. Situated in the heart of the ancient Cham Kingdom, it was in Da Nang where the French first disembarked, renaming it Tourane. Later, it was in Da Nang where the first US Marines clamoured ashore in 1965, the city serving as a pivotal US base during the **Vietnam War**.

A few miles south of Da Nang is **Hoi An**, Vietnam's earliest known port, used by the Chams who sailed up the Mekong River to trade with the Khmer and as far afield as China, Java, Malaysia, Thailand and India. During the Nguyen dynasty, the emperors allowed Hoi An a fair degree of autonomous power; by then the port town was occupied by Chinese and Japanese traders, who built houses, many of which still stand today. The prosperous port, as famous in its day during the 16th to 19th centuries as Macau or Malacca, dwindled in importance when the Thu Bon River silted up in the 19th century and port activity moved to Da Nang.

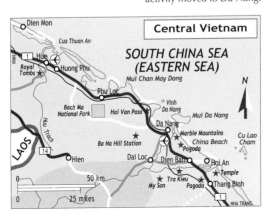

Tucked away in the hills south of Hoi An is **My Son**, the largest concentration of **monuments** standing as testament to the achievement of the Cham civilization.

HUE

Vietnam's last imperial capital, Hue, is an agreeably dispersed small city of 300,000 people lying on the banks of the **Perfume River** approximately 16km

(10 miles) from the coast. The river divides the town. On the north bank stand the walls and moats of the Citadel, which formerly enclosed the palaces, temples and gardens of the **Imperial City** and, within that, the innermost **Forbidden Purple City**. South of the river, the old French colonial quarter developed, graced by its now restored villas and tree-shaded streets. Also lining the south bank are the major hotels as well as a few streets inland where there are restaurants and banks.

When Emperor Bao Dai abdicated in 1945 with the words, 'I would rather be the citizen of an independent country than an emperor of one that is dominated', power shifted from Hue to Hanoi and Ho Chi Minh City. For all its imperial trappings, Hue found itself relegated to the role of a small provincial capital, a country cousin caught between two aggressive power blocks, the north and south. Accustomed to conservative court life laid down by tradition, Hue held to the old ways, surviving as best she could through the first rigors of **Japanese** occupation, followed by the **French Indo-China War** and then the **American War** in rapid succession.

But the old ways do have a long heritage. It is believed that the area around Hue has been occupied for at least 2000 years. Beginning as a Han Chinese military base in the 2nd century BC, the location developed as the centre of a small principality and then as one of the capitals of the Cham Kingdom. In the early 14th century, the region first became allied to the Vietnamese through

Above: *Beyond Hue and the imperial tombs, the Perfume River flows through pastoral scenery.*

RIVER EXCURSIONS

One of the most delightful ways to visit the imperial tombs is by **boat**. The city's character is largely defined by the **Perfume River** with several **major monuments**, such as Thien Mu Pagoda, being located on the river banks. Near the mouth of the river, about 12km (7.5 miles) from the city, are lagoons and Thuan An Beach, unfortunately polluted by a nearby village. Boats can be hired through tourist cafés or on the south bank just north of Tran Tien Bridge.

CHAM ALLIANCE

The region around Hue first became a part of Vietnam through a marriage alliance. In the late 13th century, the King of Champa, **Che Man**, offered two prefectures of his kingdom, **O** and **Ly**, in exchange for the hand of Viet Princess **Huyen Tran**. This laid the basis for the subsequent creation of the **Thuan Hoa** region. The romantic story might have had a sad ending when Che Man died a year after the marriage, because without the timely intervention of the Viet king, Huyen Tran would have perished on her husband's funeral pyre.

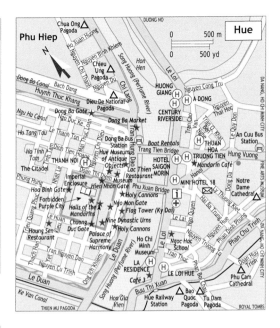

TET OFFENSIVE

On 31 January 1968, North Vietnamese forces attacked and occupied parts of Hue, including the Citadel. For the following 26 days, one of the bloodiest conflicts of the Vietnam War raged throughout the city as US and South Vietnamese forces fought bitterly to oust the invaders. Before their defeat, the Communists executed nearly 3000 civilians as 'unco-operative elements'. By US count, 142 Americans, 384 South Vietnamese and 5113 Communist troops died in the fighting, while most of Hue's imperial heritage was destroyed by rockets, bombs and artillery.

marriage, but was not fully annexed until the late 15th century. What was called **Phu Xuan**, in the 16th century, subsequently became the power centre of the Nguyen Lords, who held sway over the southern region of Vietnam for more than 200 years. Following the Tay Son rebellion, the first Nguyen emperor, Gia Long, chose the city as the **capital** of a newly unified Vietnam and in 1802, renamed it Hue.

A total of 13 successive Nguyen emperors were to rule from Hue (as titular rulers only during the French period) until the end of the dynasty in 1945. In the process they created, what is arguably, the loveliest city in the country.

Although violent episodes disrupted Hue's past, it is the pastoral harmony to which the city has always aspired that ultimately impresses the visitor. The city gains much from its lovely riverside location and you can sense a kind of serenity – a quiet, gentle, easy-going way that was once associated with old Asia, but now almost lost in the modern world.

HUE'S CITADEL ★★★

The heart of old Hue is the **Citadel**, the **Imperial City** of the **Nguyen** emperors, a city-within-a-city comprising three enclosures: the **Outer Fortification** (Kinh Thanh), the **Imperial Enclosure** (Hoang Thanh), where official functions took place, and the **Forbidden Purple City** (Tu Cam Thanh), the symbolic heart of the kingdom and the exclusive world of the immediate imperial family. Regrettably, the innermost complex was occupied by North Vietnamese troops during the 1968 Tet Offensive and in the fierce fighting to retake it, most of it was destroyed. Today, the site of the Forbidden Purple City is a huge, grassy expanse, where only the stone foundations of certain palaces can be traced. However, the few buildings that have survived or been restored within the Imperial Enclosure are sufficient to give an inkling of the Citadel's original grandeur, if not of its full former glory.

Construction of the Citadel was begun in 1804 by **Emperor Gia Long** and completed in the third decade of the century. Following a French design and mixing Oriental and Occidental **architecture**, it was the largest fortified complex ever built during the Vietnamese monarchy, nearly 10km (6 miles) in circumference and with walls 6m (20ft) high and 20m (66ft) thick, protected by a moat 23m (77ft) wide and 4m (13ft) deep. There were 10 entrances to the Citadel, each with a two-storey watchtower.

The Flag Tower (Ky Dai)

This is a substantial **monument** that served a defensive purpose, protecting the Citadel's main entrance. First erected in 1807 by **Gia Long** and later improved by his son, **Emperor Minh Mang**, it consists of three superimposed flat-topped pyramids, rising to a height of just over 17m (57ft). At the top stands a flagpole, twice increased in height, lastly to its present

Below: *Several of the 10 gates that pierce the Citadel walls have been severely damaged, but the eastern entrance still retains a colourful grandeur.*

QUOC HOC SCHOOL

Contributing to Hue's reputation as a cultural and intellectual centre is Quoc Hoc (National Studies) School at 10 Le Loi Street. Founded in 1896, this famous school's list of even more famous alumni includes former South Vietnam president Ngo Dinh Diem, General Vo Nguyen Giap, victor at Dien Bien Phu, and Ho Chi Minh, who spent a year at the school under his then name Nguyen Tat Thanh.

37m (121ft) in 1949, making it the tallest in Vietnam. Flanking the tower are the Nine Holy Cannons (four to the east and five to the west), symbols of the **Nguyen lords** – the city's guardian spirits. Cast on the orders of Gia Long and made from brass captured from the Tay Son rebels, the cannons are purely ceremonial and represent the four seasons and the five traditional elements: fire, earth, water, metal and wood.

Ngo Mon Gate (Noon or South Gate)

The main entrance to the **Imperial City** or Great Enclosure (open daily 06:30–17:30) is directly behind the Flag Tower. **Ngo Mon Gate** is one of four original gateways, the others being: the Gate of Peace (Hoa Binh) in the north, the Gate of Humanity (Hien Nhon) in the east, and the Gate of Virtue (Chuong Duc) in the west. All are monumental and ornate affairs, although Ngo Mon Gate is the largest with five doors (the others have three), the central one used exclusively by the **emperor**.

The gate is surmounted by the **Ngu Phun Pavilion** (the Pavilion of Five Phoenixes), flanked by twin belvederes. From this vantage point the emperor presided over important ceremonial occasions. The centre of the structure, where the emperor would appear, is roofed with yellow tiles, and there are green tiles on either side.

Below: *Only royal princes were allowed to stand within the walls of the Palace of Supreme Harmony, where the emperor would receive foreign emissaries during ceremonial occasions.*

Palace of Supreme Harmony (Dien Thai Hoa)

Beyond Ngo Mon Gate, a bridge (formerly only for the emperor's use) crosses a lotus pond to the **Great Rites Court** (San Dai Trieu), where court mandarins stood in attendance in order of rank. Facing this is the Palace of Supreme Harmony, the Imperial City's principal building, where court ceremonies were held and the emperor gave audiences. Measuring 44m (144ft) long and just over 30m (100ft) wide, this wooden palace was built in 1805. The interior is notable for its 80 huge red lacquered ironwood columns, carved and painted with gilt dragon and cloud designs, symbolizing the meeting of the monarch and his subjects.

Halls of the Mandarins

Facing the courtyard behind the **Palace of Supreme Harmony** are two buildings (restorations) where the mandarins used to prepare for court ceremonies (in the building on the left, visitors can pose for photographs sitting on a throne wearing royal robes). In the courtyard two 17th-century cauldrons commemorate victories of the **Nguyen Lords** over the Trinh.

The Forbidden Purple City (Tu Cam Thanh)

Once the Great Golden Gate, the most magnificent of all the Imperial City's gates, led from behind the Palace of Supreme Harmony into the inner sanctum of the Forbidden Purple City. Sadly, this gate was lost during anti-French struggles in 1947; the rest was destroyed in the **Tet Offensive** of 1968. The first building to have been restored is a small but elaborately decorated two-storey **library** (Thai Binh Lau) pavilion halfway down the east side of the compound.

Royal Theatre

The most stunning, newly rebuilt building stands off to the right from the courtyard behind the Palace of Supreme Harmony (then turn left). This dazzling new theatre is built to the original plans with thick red lacquered pillars embellished with gilt clouds and dragons. It gives one the impression of just having stepped into the glorious imperial past. Performances of traditional music and Vietnamese opera (*tuong*) take place here daily.

Back at the Palace of Supreme Harmony, following a leafy lane off to the left are several more impressive temples. Through a pretty, newly restored gate (on the left) you can see three temples standing side by side.

DYNASTY URNS

The nine dynastic urns in front of The To Mieu were cast during the reign of Minh Mang. Hundreds of craftsmen from all over the country were involved in their production. Decorated with suns, moons, dragons, mountains, natural landscapes and historic events to represent the everlasting power of the empire, the urns are estimated to weigh between 1900kg (4189lb) and 2500kg (5521lb) each.

TINH TAM LAKE

Located a short distance north of the Imperial City is Ho Tinh Tam, Lake of the Serene Heart, once a beauty spot of ancient Hue. The site is a vestige of a tributary of the Perfume River, which was diked here and broadened by Emperor Gia Long to make a rectangular lake 1.42km (0.8 miles) in circumference. Two small islands in the middle of the lake were originally occupied by storehouses for gunpowder, but Emperor Minh Mang had these removed and replaced by palaces and pavilions to become an imperial pleasure ground. Minh Mang is said to have composed 10 poems inspired by 10 views of the lake.

CONTROVERSIAL MEMORIAL

From 1807 to 1945, the Nam Giao Esplanade (Terrace of Heavenly Sacrifice) was Vietnam's most important religious site, the spot where the emperor made annual offerings to the gods to secure the nation's welfare. It is designed with three terraces, symbolizing Man, Earth and Heaven. In spite of much popular opposition, the site has been turned into a memorial to the North Vietnamese soldiers killed in the war with the South. Oddly, standing at any point on the highest platform, you can hear every spoken word from the farthest extremity. A historical site, in more ways than one, Nam Giao lies 2km (1.2 miles) south of Hue on the way to the imperial tombs.

HUE'S TRADITIONAL WATER MUSIC

Hue is known for its elegant, traditional water music and Hue singing, *Ca Hue*. To book a boat or to buy a single ticket on a boat for a romantic musical evening on the Perfume River, 49 Le Loi (behind the water puppet museum).

Hung To Mieu

The temple was built in 1804 to honour the parents of the first Nguyen emperor, Gia Long. His father, **Nguyen Phuc Luan**, had been killed in battle against the Trinhs of the north. Restored in 1997, it glistens with red lacquer. A few framed photographs are revealing as to how **feudalism** existed in Vietnam in the recent past. Duy Tan, 11th to reign, stares fixedly back from a black and white photograph. Anti-French, both he and his father, Than Thai, were exiled by the French to Reunion.

The To Mieu

First built in 1821, this building holds the funerary tablets and shrines dedicated to the first ten emperors of the Nguyen dynasty, the three serving under the French (Ham Nghi, Thanh Thai and Duy Tan), only having been added in 1959.

Nine Dynastic Urns

These ornate bronze vessels are placed in the shade of the Hien Lam Pavilion, in front of the Mieu Temple. They were cast in 1822 to symbolize the sovereignty of the dynasty and are dedicated to (the first) nine Nguyen rulers. The central and most elaborate urn is that of Gia Long, dynasty founder, who ordered them cast.

Hien Lam Pavilion

Recently rebuilt and restored, this is an elegant three-storey memorial temple dedicated, once again, to the Nguyen emperors. Pure poetry in architecture.

Minh Duong

Returning along the leafy lane, turn to the left for another complex under restoration.

This surprisingly unroyal 19th-century French-style **villa** (Minh Duong) – with a wrap-around porch (not open) – first served the queen mother and first wife of Emperor Dong Khan, **Empress Thanh Cung**, as a private clinic. Later it became the residence of the last emperor, Bao Dai. Beyond are two courtyards surrounded by temples under restoration.

Truong An Gate

Continuing north along the leafy lane, Truong An is the most charming gate in the Citadel. Built in 1822, it was listed in 1844 as one of the twenty most beautiful spots in Hue by Emperor Thieu Tri, known for his poetry. Inside, beyond the dancing tortoises and unicorns made of blue-and-white china, the crescent-shaped lake and island rockery of the pleasure gardens are a long-term restoration project.

Above: *The nine dynastic urns commemorating the first nine Nguyen emperors stand beside Hien Lam Pavilion in the Citadel in Hue.*

BEYOND HUE'S CITADEL

Lively **Dong Ba Market**, on Tran Hung Dao Street, is on the north bank of the river next to the bus station. It is best to visit early in the morning when the fish come in.

Dieu De National Pagoda

Located at 102 Bach Dang Street, directly east of the Citadel, is a pagoda distinguished by its four towers. It was formerly under the direct patronage of the emperor, hence 'national'. In the 60s, it was a hotbed of Buddhist opposition to the war and the South Vietnamese government and it was raided by the police in 1966.

Chua Ong Pagoda

A little way to the north, this large Chinese Buddhist pagoda dates from the 19th century. It has a somewhat interesting interior, although the building was badly damaged during the **Tet Offensive**.

Tin Lanh

The only church on the north bank of the river, stands a short distance northeast of Dieu De National Pagoda.

Quang Pagoda

On Nguyen Chi Thanh Street, is Hue's largest Theravada Buddhist temple. Although the building is modern, its Sri

---

NGUYEN DYNASTY

Gia Long: 1802–19
Minh Mang: 1820–40
Thieu Tri: 1840–47
Tu Duc: 1848–83
Duc Duc: 1883 (dethroned after three days)
Hiep Hoa: 1883 (assassinated)
Kien Phuc: 1883–84
Ham Nghi: 1884–85 (dethroned)
Dong Khan: 1885–89
Than Thai: 1889–1907 (deposed)
Duy Tan: 1907–16 (deposed)
Khai Dinh: 1916–25
Bao Dai: 1925–45 (abdicated)

Lankan-influenced architecture sets it apart from the horizontal style of Mahayana Buddhist pagodas.

Thien Mu Pagoda
(Pagoda of the Heavenly Lady) ★★★

Standing in splendid isolation on a hillock overlooking the Perfume River some 4km (2.5 miles) upstream from the Citadel, this is one of Vietnam's most famous sights. Legend has it that the pagoda was founded in 1601 after an old woman dressed in a red gown and green trousers appeared on the hill and prophesied: 'Soon a true king will come here and build a pagoda that will attract and converge all the heavenly forces and energies of the Dragon Veins.' After having uttered these words the woman vanished. Accepting the prophesy as his destiny, Lord Nguyen Hoang, the first of ten Nguyen feudal lords to rule over the area during the 17th and 18th centuries, built a pagoda, which he named 'Heavenly Lady'. None of his original buildings survive; those seen today date from works carried out in 1714–15 and 1844–46.

Dominating the entire compound is the wedding-cake architecture of the seven-storey Phuoc Duyen Tower, 21m (69ft) high, built by Emperor Thieu Tri in 1844. Each storey represents an incarnation of the Buddha. Beside the tower is the main sanctuary dominated by an enormous **laughing Buddha**. The sanctuary also contains a stele carved in 1715, set on the back of a marble tortoise. A pavilion on the left houses a huge bell cast in 1710, weighing over two tons. Nearby are shrines to Quan Vo (God of War) and Quan An (Goddess of Mercy). The site commands splendid views out over the Perfume River, especially when the flamboyant trees are blooming. Services are at dawn and 16:00. It is also a good place to buy **paintings** on silk.

SOUTH OF HUE'S RIVER

The area once known as the 'New City', the French quarter, with its wide boulevards, spacious villas, new hotels, restaurants and government buildings, feels quite modern by comparison.

FIERY PROTEST

On 11 June 1963, Thich Quang Duc, a 73-year-old monk from Thien Mu Pagoda, immolated himself in Ho Chi Minh City to protest at the Ngo Dinh Diem government's persecution of Buddhists. The event, making world headlines in a famous press photograph, set an example for the self-immolation of other monks and nuns, and accelerated the downfall of Diem, who was killed in a military coup on 2 November. The Austin car in which Thich Quang Duc drove to Ho Chi Minh City is preserved in a building behind Thien Mu Pagoda's main sanctuary.

Bao Quoc Pagoda

A pagoda has existed on this site off Dien Bien Phu Street since 1670, although there have been numerous renovations. Several buildings occupy the garden-like complex where there are also monks' tombs.

Tu Dam Pagoda

On Dien Bien Phu Street, a short distance south of Bao Quoc, Tu Dam pagoda derives its reputation from a tradition of militant Buddhism. The pagoda was the centre of a reformed school of **Buddhism**, originating in China in the 1920s, and it was here that the Unified Vietnamese Buddhist Association was formed in the 1950s. During the following decade, the pagoda was a centre of opposition to President Diem and the war. In 1968, it was a target of the North Vietnamese forces during their Tet Offensive.

Phu Cam Cathedral

East of Tu Dam Pagoda is the headquarters of the **Hue diocese**. A church has existed on the site since the 17th century. Construction of the present building begun in 1963, although it was left unfinished when work was halted in 1975.

Notre Dame Cathedral

Hue's other cathedral on Nguyen Hue Street is well worth seeking out for its curious architecture, which mixes monumental European and Oriental styles – notice the three-tiered pagoda-like spire. Although dating from the mid-20th century, the building is wonderfully self-assured.

HUE'S IMPERIAL TOMBS ★★★

The royal tombs – think of pleasure grounds and temples rather than cemeteries and mausoleums – of the Nguyen emperors who ruled in Hue from 1802 to 1945, are located south of the city amidst picturesque wooded hills on both sides of the Perfume River. Combining park-like landscapes and lakes with certain traditional

Opposite: *The seven-storey tower of Thien Mu Pagoda measures 21m (69ft), each storey containing an altar to a different Buddha.*
Below: *The graceful interior of Hue's Catholic Cathedral.*

HO CHI MINH TRAIL

A major factor in the North's war effort and a symbol of the Communists' determination, the Ho Chi Minh Trail was not a single path but rather a 15,000km (9300-mile) network of secret and camouflaged tracks. Along this vital conduit, the North Vietnamese shipped arms and equipment to their guerrilla comrades in the South, initially by bicycle and later by truck. A section of the trail runs through the west of Da Nang from where excursions can be arranged – check with hotel or local tour agencies.

architectural elements, each tomb is an extensive affair comprising this sequence: a pavilion housing a stele recording the emperor's achievements; a brick-paved court of honour where life-sized stone mandarins and animal figures stand in attendance; a temple of the soul enshrining the funerary tablet and precious objects belonging to the emperor; a mausoleum and additional houses for guards, servants and retainers. Although they follow a general traditional pattern, most of the tombs were designed and built during their future occupants' lifetimes and so display variations that reflect their different characters and personalities.

The tombs are spread out over a wide area and can be visited by boat or bus tour, by taxi, motorbike or bike. Included on the tours are:

The Tomb of Khai Dinh

Located about 10km (6 miles) south of Hue, this tomb is hardly the most representative, but must be seen for comparison. The Vietnamese don't like it very much. It eschews all efforts at Oriental restraint and makes a delirious bid for immortality through a huge, garish baroque creation. Emperor Khai Dinh ruled from 1916 to 1925 and his tomb was built between 1920 and 1931, much influenced by his notion of European grandeur. The approach is up three steep flights of dragon-flanked steps, which open onto an expanse of statue-studded courtyard. The *pièce de résistance* is the interior of the mausoleum, a claustrophobic extravaganza of porcelain and glass mosaic, and the tomb itself is topped by a larger-than-life gilt statue of Khai Dinh himself. A masterpiece of kitsch on a grand scale.

Below: *Stone mandarins stand in permanent attendance in the court of honour at Khai Dinh's tomb.*

The Tomb of Minh Mang

About 12km (7.5 miles) from Hue, Minh Mang's tomb is on the opposite river bank (there's a bridge). Minh Mang, possibly the greatest of the Nguyen emperors, ruled from 1820 to

1840 and his tomb was completed in 1843. His burial site comprises classical architectural forms, methodically and harmoniously laid out in a satisfyingly tranquil landscaped setting of lotus ponds, flowering trees and lakes. Combining solemnity with symmetry, the tomb is set within an oval-walled enclosure. Along the east-west axis, running 700m (765yd) from the main gate, are the principal features: the court of honour, the

stele pavilion, Hien Duc Gate, Sung An Temple, Hoang Trach Gate, Trung Dao Bridge, Minh Law Pavilion (atop a three-tiered terrace) and, beyond a crescent-shaped lake, the circular walled burial mound.

Above: *Minh Mang's tomb blends the beauty of its natural setting with majestic architecture and exquisite stone sculpture.*

The Tomb of Tu Duc

Tu Duc ruled from 1848 to 1883 – the Nguyen dynasty's longest reign. The tomb, located about 8km (5 miles) from Hue on the south bank, was built between 1864 and 1867 in what was then tiger infested jungle. It was designed by the emperor as a secluded poetic fairyland where he could write poetry and enjoy life's pleasures and, in death, find a harmonious resting place. Comprising some 50 structures enclosed by a 1500m (1640yd) wall, the tomb is entered via the Vu Khiem Gate in the south. To the right is the delightful Luu Khiem Lake, with Tinh Khiem islet in the middle. Straight ahead is the Du Khiem Pavilion and, across the lake, Xung Khiem Pavilion – built over the water on stilts – where Tu Duc used to sit and compose poetry. West of Du Khiem Pavilion is the Hoa Khiem Temple (used as a palace during Tu Duc's lifetime), and a complex of buildings, including, on the right, Minh Khiem royal theatre. The

HILL STATION

A cool retreat from Hue is offered by Mt Bach Ma, an old French hill station, now a national park, located some 55km (34 miles) southwest of the city. Situated at an altitude of more than 1400m (4590ft), Bach Ma is reported to hold 125 species of wildlife, including more than 800 species of birds. Bach Ma offers walking trails and fine views amid lush greenery and a year-round spring-like climate. Facilities are few and at present you must hire a guide. Best from February to September.

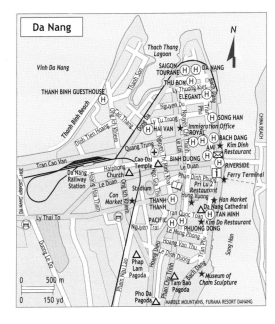

Da Nang

court of honour, stele pavilion and mausoleum are directly to the north of the Hoa Khiem Temple complex, although the emperor's mortal remains are not here; the site of his burial is unknown. Fine landscaping and an atmosphere of oriental fantasy distinguish the site.

DA NANG

An exceptional natural setting has given Da Nang its historic importance, while its relative distance from political power centres has assured a certain individuality. Da Nang is Vietnam's fourth-largest city with a population of 890,500 and it lies 754km (471 miles) south of Hanoi and 944km (580 miles) north of Ho Chi Minh City. Hue is only about 100km (62 miles) to the north, separated by the Hai Van Pass, a natural divide, geographically and meteorologically.

The port city sits on the west bank of the mouth of the Han River, which flows out into a horseshoe bay. Protected from the South China Sea by a spur of land on the west and a broadly curving coastline to the east, the bay is a huge and perfect natural harbour.

Hoi An (*see* page 76) was originally the region's principal **port** and centre of foreign trade. Da Nang first became known in the 17th and 18th centuries as the gateway – and later a battleground – for the first European arrivals, the Portuguese, followed by the Dutch and the French. Rechristened Tourane by the French, Da Nang became a French trade concession area in 1787.

In the 19th century Da Nang succeeded Hoi An as Central Vietnam's major port. In 1847, it entered another

HUE'S FESTIVALS

Every two years (2010, 2012, etc.) in early June Hue stages an international cultural festival. Royal court ceremonies are staged at the Citadel and numerous countries participate, sending performers. *See* www.huefestival.com

phase of history when a French man-of-war sailed into the harbour, thereby sparking the struggle for colonial acquisition. The original intention had been to land at Hue, but the river estuary was too shallow for the French ships.

Major development of Da Nang began after the partition of the country in 1954. A decade later the place became famous as the spot where the first US combat troops to arrive in Vietnam landed on 8 March 1965. The port was subsequently transformed into a huge American naval and air base (with the longest jet aircraft runway in Southeast Asia). As such an important **military target**, Da Nang drew so much enemy fire that it became known as 'Rocket City'.

Today most visitors bypass staying in Da Nang in favour of delightful Hoi An, nipping into the Museum of Cham Sculpture on arrival or departure.

Museum of Cham Sculpture (Bao Tang Cham) ★★★

Da Nang's one not-to-be-missed sight is the museum of Cham Sculpture, located in the southern part of the city at the corner of Tran Phu and Le Dinh Duong Streets. Da Nang lies at the centre of the area once dominated by the Chams and the museum houses one of the world's finest collections of Cham sculpture (visit also the Guimet Museum in Paris and the History Museums in Hanoi and Ho Chi Minh City). Open daily from 07:30 to 11:00 and 13:30 to 16:30.

Marvellously accomplished sandstone carvings of gods, goddesses, beasts and celestial dancing girls are a glorious testament to the great artistic talents of the Chams.

Opened in 1916 under the patronage of the very highly respected Ecole Française d'Extrème Orient and enlarged in 1936, the museum has approximately 300 exhibits dating from the 7th to the 15th centuries. According to legend, the Chams sprang from

> **CHAM ARCHITECTURE**
>
> Brick was the prime medium of Cham architecture. Of excellent quality, the bricks were rubbed smooth and finely bonded with a mortar made from vegetable matter. Temples consist essentially of a tall, square sanctuary tower, a square entrance hall and a steep roof of several storeys in descending size. Pilasters and projections give the towers their characteristic graceful proportions. Smaller attendant buildings included libraries usually with corbelled brick roofs and halls.

Below: *Da Nang's airy Museum of Cham Sculpture has some fine exhibits, dating from the 7th to the 15th century.*

Uroja – the mother goddess. She was one of a trinity of deities although she was the only goddess. She is also confusingly known as Po Nagar. In the Cham language her name translates as 'woman's breast', which explains the abundance of rounded breasts used as borders around the friezes and pedestals. Much influenced by **Hinduism** and later **Buddhism**, the Chams adopted **Sanskrit** as a religious language. Their own language originated from Malayo-Polynesian roots and to this day the Chams around Phan Rang, further south, speak a language related to one spoken by a tribe in Borneo. A worthwhile booklet on sale at the museum, written by former director Tran Ky Phuong, provides a good general introduction to Cham art.

BEST BEACHES

China Beach is Da Nang's best beach, situated about 14km (8.5 miles) south of the city. This 20km (12-mile) sandy beach was used for rest and recreation during the Vietnam War and it was made famous by a US TV series of the same name. **Lang Co** is an idyllic spot with all the right ingredients – an unspoilt fishing village,a blue lagoon and a sandy beach – and it is located about 40km (25 miles) north of Da Nang. **Nam O Beach** lies about 15km (9 miles) north of Da Nang. **Thanh Binh Beach** is the closest to Da Nang at 2km (1.5 miles), but it is usually crowded and therefore not recommended. **My Khe Beach**, about 6km (4 miles) from central Da Nang, is a better beach but an undertow makes swimming unsafe.

Other City Sights

The following attractions can easily be covered on a walking tour heading west, and then heading north from the Museum.

Tam Bao Pagoda, at 253 Phan Chu Trinh Street, is a Theravada Buddhist pagoda, the only one in Da Nang, distinguished by a five-tiered tower and 'begging monks', who wear brown robes. Inside on the right is an emaciated begging Buddha, on the left a seated Buddha.

Pho Da Pagoda, at 340 Phan Chu Trinh Street, is a pretty yellow pagoda with a graceful three-tiered yellow and green tiled roof. A large 'gold' statue of Buddha dominates the interior. This particular incarnation, **Thich Ca Mu Ni**, sits amongst statues of bodhisattvas, those who have attained Nirvana, but chose to remain in this world to help others along the way.

Phap Lam Pagoda, at 574 Ong Ich Khiem Street, looks quite old with its mossy tiled roof, but it was built in

1934. A serene statue of Quan Am, Goddess of Mercy, presides over the garden and seated in her own tiny pavilion is the figure of a highly colourful, multi-armed goddess, Thien Nhon.

Da Nang Cathedral, on Tran Phu Street, about four blocks north of the Cham Museum, was built in 1923. It is a delightful pink and white Gothic confection that looks like something turned out by Wedgewood.

Cao Dai Temple, on Haiphong Street, is the second largest Cao Dai Temple in Vietnam (after Tay Ninh). From the huge altarpiece globe, the characteristic 'divine eye', the religion's symbol, stares out at the worshippers. A sign translates as 'All religions have the same reason'.

AROUND DA NANG
Marble Mountains (Ngu Hanh Son)
About 12km (7.5 miles) south of Da Nang, five extraordinary hills rise from the coastal plain. They are actually limestone with marble outcrops and each is dedicated to one of the five traditional elements: water (*thuy son*), fire (*hoa son*), earth (*tho son*), metal or gold (*kim son*) and wood (*moc son*). The spot has been sacred since the time of the Chams when grottoes in the hills were turned into first Hindu and, then later, Buddhist shrines.

The hill most visited is Thuy Son. You need to be a bit of a mountain goat to negotiate the steps, although children are always on hand to act as guides.

Atmospheric with their looming statuary shrouded in incense smoke, the main sights on Thuy Son are Linh Ung Pagoda, **Tam Thai Pagoda** (built by Emperor Minh Mang in 1825) and the spectacularly cavernous **Huyen Khong Cave**, a site of Buddhist pilgrimage. Hoa Hai village at the foot of the mountains specializes in carved marble statues and inexpensive souvenirs. Many prefer to watch the craftsmen at work rather than climb the mountain.

> **COOL ESCAPE**
>
> Located about 45km (28 miles) west of Da Nang is **Ba Na**, once a hill retreat where French colonials escaped the summer heat. The scenery and views are magnificent, while the 1460m (4790ft) altitude ensures cool temperatures. There are now three hotels to choose from, reached via the Ba Na Resort cable car, tel: 511 379 1791, rsvn@banahills.com.vn

Opposite: *An uninterrupted stretch of sand and sea, China Beach, at the foot of the Marble Mountains, was once a 'Rest and Relaxation' spot for US military personnel during the Vietnam War.*
Below: *One of the five Marble Mountains contained a field hospital that was bombed, leaving a hole open to the sky.*

HOI AN AND AROUND

Hoi An has an embarrassment of small cafés and restaurants, which makes it a good spot for lingering. A delightful excursion can be taken from Hoi An to nearby Cau Dai Beach, an easy bike or mototaxi ride some 5km (3 miles) east of town down Tran Hung Dao Street. The beach has fine white sand and the water is clear and good for bathing.

Below: *An important 16th-century trading port on the route between China and India, Hoi An is now a tranquil town on the banks of the Thu Bon River.*

Hoi An

Situated on the banks of the Thu Bon River 30km (19 miles) south of Da Nang, the little town of Hoi An (known to the Chinese as Faifo) feels caught in a time warp. It is filled with the atmosphere of centuries past. This one-time international trading port, now a quaint backwater, has an impressive heritage.

Archaeologists believe the site to have been inhabited for at least 2000 years, while its history as a seaport reaches back to the 2nd century AD, when it was the principal port for Champa. A fresh lease of life arrived in the 16th century when a wave of Chinese and Japanese settlers established Hoi An as a port of call on the China–India trade route. Then came European merchants and missionaries, first the Portuguese, later the Dutch, Spanish, French and British, who called in at Hoi An to purchase high-grade silk, herbal medicines, mother-of-pearl, areca nuts, lacquer, porcelain and other exotic cargoes.

Although badly damaged during the **Tay Son rebellion** in the late 18th century, Hoi An had flourished as one of Southeast Asia's most important ports until the 19th century when the **Thu Bon River** silted up and prevented the passage of ocean-going vessels. Hoi An's economic clock stopped, which resulted in how much the town appears today as it must have done a century or more ago – preserved like a fly in amber.

Declared a **World Heritage Site** by UNESCO, the wise local authorities have claimed the entire town a pedestrian area – with the exception of bikes, *cyclos* (bicycle trishaws) and motorbikes. The traditional temples, shrines, Chinese communal houses and a few private houses are open to the public with a ticket that includes a choice of several. To visit them all, simply buy two, or even three tickets. Narrow streets, huddled wooden shophouses and a corrugated skyline of crusty

tiled roofs smothered in morning glories exude antiquity. Furthermore, Hoi An probably offers the best, most concentrated shopping street in all of Vietnam for all manner of crafts, antiques, clothes, silk, lacquer, ceramics, bronze and wood statues, embroidery, marble and jade jewellery. Add a plethora of excellent tiny restaurants, some overlooking the river, and Hoi An appeals as an exciting place to linger.

Sightseeing in Hoi An ★★★

Hoi An, with its lively old houses, plethora of restaurants and delightful shops, cannot be done in a day. Stay over to absorb the town's atmosphere and genuine charm. The town is small and best explored on foot (or *cyclo*), with most major sights on or near **Tran Phu Street**, the main east–west artery running parallel to, and a couple of blocks back from, the waterfront. The following is a suggested walking tour starting near the market.

Above: *Chinese influence can be seen in the ornamental detail of Hoi An's domestic architecture.*

Quan Cong Temple and **Quan Am Pagoda** stand back to back at the corner of Nguyen Hue and Tran Phu Streets, opposite the market. Dating from the mid-17th century, these are small but atmospheric Chinese temples enclosed around a central courtyard. The former is dedicated to legendary Chinese warrior Quan Cong, whose large and colourful papier-mâché statue is flanked by those of one of his generals, **Chau Xuong**, and a mandarin, **Quan Binh**.

Situated across the street is lively **Hoi An Market**, extending down to the river and selling dry goods as well as fresh produce.

East from Quan Cong Temple are two Chinese assembly halls (where Tran Phu Street becomes Nguyen Duy Hieu Street). Hai Nam Assembly Hall was built in 1883 and it has an ornate interior. A bit further east, beyond the intersection with Hoang Dieu Street, the Trieu Chau Assembly Hall is a 200-year-old building with some exceptional woodcarving.

Retracing one's steps back west along Tran Phu Street, the **Fukien Chinese Assembly Hall** stands opposite 35 Tran Phu Street. Dating originally from the late 17th century, and rebuilt at the end of the 19th, the hall is

KHE SANH

In early 1968, the USA feared its base at Khe Sanh, south of the DMZ (Demilitarized Zone) near Huong Hoa, could become another Dien Bien Phu, and reinforced it accordingly. Although not defeated, Khe Sanh was besieged for 77 days in one of the bloodiest – and arguably most pointless – battles of the war. As many as 500 US Marines and 10,000–15,000 North Vietnamese were killed; 67,500 metric tons of bombs were dropped in the area, and buried explosives are still killing people at Khe Sanh today.

Above: *The graceful curve of the Japanese Covered Bridge suggests the movement of the waters beneath.*

Below: *A neatly dressed schoolteacher on her way to class in Hoi An.*

dedicated to Thien Hau, Goddess of the Sea.

The house at 77 Tran Phu Street is a fine and well-preserved example of Hoi An's domestic architecture of some 300 years ago. It is still a private house but open to visitors.

Towards the western end of Tran Phu Street, just beyond the intersection with Nhi Trung Street, is the 18th-century assembly hall dedicated to **Quang Dong**. At the end of the street is Japanese Covered Bridge, an 18m (60ft) wooden structure built at the end of the 16th century by the Japanese community. The eastern and western ends of the bridge are flanked by statues of a pair of monkeys and a pair of dogs, placed here because construction of the bridge was begun in the Year of the Monkey and was completed in the Year of the Dog. There is a tiny pagoda hidden within the bridge.

Tan Ky House, at 101 Nguyen Thai Hoc Street, is a sumptuous traditional old house. It has been, one might say, sculpted of local hard wood, its well-preserved architecture and antique decoration offering a glimpse of how prosperous Hoi An merchants lived a century or more ago. This private house, open to visitors, has elegant inlaid mother-of-pearl columns decorated in a delightful floral design.

From Nguyen Thai Hoc Street, it is a short walk to the charming little waterfront where boats can be hired for the trip across the river to **Cam Kim Island**, long renowned for its boat builders and woodcarvers. Here, there is a project to train young people to carve in the age-old tradition. It is well worth visiting.

On the northern outskirts of town, **Chuc Thanh Pagoda** is a restored version of Hoi An's oldest temple, originally founded in 1454. Beyond Chuc Thanh stands **Phuoc Lam Pagoda**, which dates from the 17th century.

My Son ★★

Hidden away in a secret valley, My Son represents the most extensive Cham **ruins** in Vietnam. Thought to have been an important Cham intellectual and religious centre and possibly the burial place of Cham kings, it was named a **World Heritage Site** in 2000 by UNESCO. Bearing in mind that during the Vietnam War, My Son was used as a Viet Cong field headquarters and therefore attracted heavy bombing (until a curator of the Guimet Museum in Paris sent a plea to President Nixon to stop the bombing) and the surrounding area was heavily mined, it is somewhat surprising that as much remains as there is.

Of the 68 **monuments** built at My Son, fewer than 20 remain standing. Some restoration work has been done and more is planned. It is nevertheless thought-provoking to wander amongst the red brick ruins of towers and temples, some built as early as the 8th century.

Honouring **Hindu** divinities, particularly Siva, and dedicated to Cham kings, the most characteristic structures are towers with four porticoes. The towers display fine brickwork, along with stone sculpture, bas-relief carvings and other rather highly accomplished decorative work. Ingeniously, bricks were rubbed smooth against one another to make a tight fit and glued together using a tree sap instead of mortar, the same tree sap that is still used to seal boats.

Set in a river valley surrounded by hills, the monuments of My Son comprise 10 main groups, which archaeologists have designated by letters and divided by numbers. Most rewarding are the two adjacent temple complexes (originally square enclosures) titled B and C. The former is the larger and although only the base of the main sanctuary remains, the smaller attendant buildings are comparatively well preserved.

My Son is located about 60km (37 miles) south of Da Nang and west of Tra Kieu. The site is no longer difficult to reach. Day tours can be arranged through Da Nang or Hoi An hotels or travel agents. Tours go in the morning. To have the ruins to yourself, go in the afternoon by taxi or motorbike and take an umbrella – it's very hot.

Above: *The Chams honoured Hindu divinities, as the sinuous curves of this stone carving show.*

CHAM CAPITALS

Tra Kieu was the site of Simhapura (Lion Citadel), Cham capital from the 4th to the 8th centuries, although only traces of the ramparts can be seen today. Some 20km (12 miles) from My Son, Dong Duong was the city of Indrapura, the 9th- to 10th-century Cham capital and site of an important late 9th-century Buddhist monastery.

Central Vietnam at a Glance

BEST TIMES TO VISIT

Dec–Mar is generally best for Central Vietnam. Hue is best from **Feb–Jun**.

GETTING THERE

Hue is served by domestic flights from Hanoi, Ho Chi Minh City and Da Nang. **Da Nang** receives international flights from Bangkok, Hong Kong and Singapore; domestic flights from Ho Chi Minh City, Nha Trang, Hue and Hanoi. The Hanoi–Ho Chi Minh City **railway links** Hue and Da Nang. **Hoi An** is reached by **taxi** or **bus** from Da Nang, 30km (18 miles).

GETTING AROUND

Bicycles, *cyclos* and metered **taxis** are readily available.

WHERE TO STAY

Hue
LUXURY
La Residence, 5 Le Loi Street, tel: 54 383 7475, resa@la-residence-hue.com www.la-residence-hue.com Newly renovated residence of the former French Governor on the bank of the Perfume River. **Hotel Saigon Morin**, 30 Le Loi Street, tel: 54 382 3526, fax: 54 382 5155, info@morinhotel.com.vn www.morinhotel.com.vn Lovely huge rooms overlooking gardens and the river.

MID-RANGE
Huong Giang Hotel, 51 Le Loi Street, tel: 54 382 2122, fax: 54 382 3123,

info@huonggianghotel.com.vn www.huonggianghotel.com The best riverside location for boat watching. Exotic imperial Hue-style decor, a new wing and a casino. Foreigners only. **Asia Hotel**, 17 Pham Ngu Lao Street, tel: 54 383 0283, info @asiahotel.com.vn www.asia hotel.com.vn Prize-winning hotel with pool and luxury features at half the price, near restaurants and the river.

BUDGET
Hoa Hong Hotel, 01 Pham Ngu Lao Street, tel: 54 382 4377, hoahonghotel@gmail. com www.hoahonghotel. com.vn A large, traditional hotel. Good value.
Binh Duong Hotel 2, 8 Ngo Gia Tue, tel: 54 384 6466, binhduong2@dng.vnn.vn A large variety of rooms here, located in a residential neighbourhood, not far from the central tourist area.

Da Nang
LUXURY
Furama Resort Da Nang, 68 Ho Xuan Huong (China Beach), tel: 511 384 7333, fax: 511 384 7666, reservation@furama vietnam.com www.furama vietnam.com On beach, a few kilometres from town. Vietnam's first five-star resort.

Hoi An
Warning: It gets tightly booked around Tet (*see* page 126).
LUXURY
Victoria Hoi An Resort, Cua Dai Beach, tel: 510 392

7040, resa.hoian@victoria hotels-asia.com Still the most luxurious hotel on the beach: sea or river views, hardwood floors and furniture and elephant rides. **Hoi An Riverside Resort & Spa**, 175 Cua Dai Road, tel: 510 386 4800, fax: 510 386 4900, sales@hoianriverresort. com.vn www.hoianriver resort.com Really charming hotel in tropical gardens, superb views of paddies, river and sea.
Hoi An Beach Resort, 01 Cua Dai Road, tel: 510 392 7011, fax: 510 392 7019, reservation @hoianbeachresort.com.vn www.hoianbeachresort.com.vn A younger and more elegant sister of the hotel in town.

MID-RANGE
Hoi An Hotel, 10 Tran Hung Dao Street, Hoi An Town, tel: 510 386 1445, resa@hoian hotel.com.vn www.hoian tourist.com This lovely old French colonial hotel is the classiest in town. Nice pool and a seductive new Zen spa. **Thuy Duong 3**, 92094 Ba Trieu Street, tel: 510 391 6565, thuyduongco@dng.vnn.vn www.thuyduonghotel-hoian. com A luxurious new in-town hotel, built around an elegant colonnaded courtyard pool. **Vinh Hung III**, 96 Ba Triu St, tel: 510 391 6277 or 391 7277, sales@vinhhung3hotel.com www.vinhhung3hotel.com The newest incarnation of this hotel group, next door to Thuy Duong.

Central Vietnam at a Glance

Vinh Hung II, Nhi Trung St, tel: 510 386 4074 or 391 0393, vinhhung.ha@dng.vnn.vn www.vinhhunghotels.com.vn This slightly older sister hotel to Vinh Hung III offers great value and a pool.

Thanh Binh II, 712 Hai Ba Trung Street, tel: 510 391 6363, vothlhong@dng.vnn.vn The eight-year-old sister hotel of Thanh Binh II offers a pool, tubs, cable TV and Internet.

Hue

Hue has a number of interesting local specialities: *banh beo*, *ram*, and *banh khoai*.

Mme Ton Nu Ha's Tinh Gia Vien Restaurant, 7K/28 Le Thanh Ton Street, tel/fax: 54 522 243, tinhgiavien@dng.vnn.vn Serves ten-course banquets in the imperial style in a garden setting. Presentation is unique. Food is literally sculpted by artist chef Mme Ton Nu Ha. Vegetarian meals, cookery classes on request.

Huong Giang Hotel, tel: 54 382 2122. Serves good Vietnamese and Western food in top-floor restaurant overlooking the river. Its ground floor restaurants stages imperial banquets in costume with traditional music.

The Tropical Garden Restaurant, 27 Chu Van An Street, tel: 510 391 1227. Live traditional Vietnamese music every evening and

excellent Vietnamese and Western food.

La Carambole, 19 Pham Ngu Lao, tel: 54 381 0491. This friendly bistro-type restaurant, owned by a Frenchman and his Vietnamese wife, serves both Western and Vietnamese food.

Mediterraneo, 2 Ben Nghe, tel: 54 381 9849. Same excellent home-made pasta at this new sister restaurant as in Hanoi.

Hoi An

The Cargo Club Restaurant and Hoi An Patisserie, 107-109 Nguyen Thai Hoc Hoi An, tel: 510 391 1227, info@cargo-hoian.com www.hoian hospitality.com Superb food and French pastries, upstairs terrace with a river view.

Bazar Café & Restaurant, 36 Tran Phu St, tel: 510 391 1229, info@bazarcafe.net www.bazarcafe.net Scrumptious Vietnamese food and barbecues in the garden of this stylish historic house furnished with antiques.

Miss Ly, 22 Nguyen Hue St, tel: 510 386 1603, lycafe22@ yahoo.com For years Miss Ly and her mother have served great Vietnamese food in this lovely old house.

Hoi An

Hoi An is a paradise for shopaholics – tailors have an international reputation, excellent at copying.

Hue

Vidotour Hue, 10 Tran Thuc Nhan Street, Hue, tel: 54 382 4813, hue@vidotourtravel.com There are also excursions from Hue to Vietnam War sites.

Sinh Café, 7 Nguyen Tri Phuong St, tel: 54 382 4813, sinhcafetour@hn.vnn.vn

Mandarin Café, 24 Tran Cao Van Street, tel: 54 382 1281, mandarin@dng.vnn.vn www.mrcumandarin.com Apart from tours, do have a look at Mr Cu's fine photos of Vietnamese life.

Hoi An

Any hotel can arrange excursions to **My Son**.

Da Nang Family Medical Practice, 50–52 Nguyen Van Linh Street, Nam Duong Ward, Hai Chau District, tel: 511 358 2699, danang@vietnammedical practice.com

HUE	J	F	M	A	M	J	J	A	S	O	N	D
AVERAGE TEMP. °F	70	72	75	79	82	84	84	84	87	78	75	71
AVERAGE TEMP. °C	21	21	24	26	28	29	29	29	27	26	24	22
RAINFALL in	3	1	1	1	2	3	3	4	14	24	14	8
RAINFALL mm	96	33	22	27	62	87	85	103	350	613	366	299
DAYS OF RAINFALL	14	7	5	6	9	8	9	4	15	21	21	19

5
Nha Trang and the Central Highlands

Most people fly the 540km (337 miles) south from Da Nang to the beach resort of **Nha Trang**. You sacrifice some fine undeveloped beaches and a few Cham towers along the way, but it is easier to fly in, sit back and relax on the beach for a few days, and then think about excursions to the hill **tribes** of the Central Highlands (who still call themselves *montagnards*, as they were once referred to by the French).

In the past few years, Nha Trang has grown beyond all recognition from a sleepy fishing town with one idyllic resort and a dozen small hotels to a bustling beach town boasting over 100 hotels.

Vying with the **sea** for attention, however, are the **mountains**. Lying all along Vietnam's narrow coastal plain, the Truong Son Mountains make their presence felt. Although the **Central Highlands** are sparsely populated, the area has always been strategically important. Despite much of the hard wood forests having been either destroyed by Agent Orange during the Vietnam War or cleared for farming, a quarter of a century later, the lush greenness has now returned.

Buon Ma Thuot, north of Nha Trang (or fly to Buon Ma Thuot directly from Ho Chi Minh City), is the largest city in the western highlands and it lies in a coffee-growing area surrounded by a scattering of *montagnards* villages. Still further north, the town of Kon Tum itself contains certain neighbourhoods occupied by *montagnards*.

At the southern end of the Truong Son range, **Da Lat** is the hill station that the French playfully dubbed 'La Petite

DON'T MISS

*** Nha Trang:** see Cham towers and tropical beaches.
** Water sports:** experience snorkelling and diving amongst the coral in Nha Trang.
* Hon Chong Promontory:** visit this popular beauty spot near Nha Trang.
* Ngoan Muc Pass:** capture vertiginous views on this panoramic mountain road.
** Da Lat:** take a cool break in the highlands.

Opposite: *Sun, sea and sand – the palm-fringed beach of Nha Trang.*

CLIMATE

The climate is warmer, less humid and generally more tropical further south, except in the almost temperate Central Highlands, where it is cooler, even cold, from November to February. Unlike the rest of southern Vietnam, Nha Trang gets most of its rain during October and November. The rains, however, are rarely prolonged and usually limited to short, sharp spells, even during the wettest months. The dry season is from June to October.

Paris', a wonderful anomaly, complete with its own colourfully lit Eiffel Tower. A favourite honeymoon destination of the Vietnamese, the town is built around a small lake, surrounded by a fertile upland region of rugged scenic beauty with forested hills, calm and enchanting lakes, and beautiful waterfalls.

NHA TRANG

A gently curving bay, a clear, warm turquoise sea and a superb beach of 6km (4 miles), plus a historical site or two, make Nha Trang the current most popular seaside destination in Vietnam. Fifteen years ago Nha Trang felt like a big rustic village, with only one luxury beach resort and a dozen indifferent hotels.

Today the bumpy road along the beach has become a **boulevard** and a palm-lined **promenade**. On the beach you can get a massage, a pedicure or a beauty treatment. More than 100 hotels, a few luxurious, line the promenade and dot the streets inland. Numerous restaurants offer international cuisine. Nha Trang's population has soared to nearly 350,000, and added to foreign visitors, the Vietnamese have discovered their own favourite beach resort.

Thanks to a huge fishing fleet of 10,000 trawlers in this region, Nha Trang is the **seafood** capital of Vietnam. On the northern side of town, beyond the new hotels facing

Below: *Market traders rendezvous at an early morning fish market in Nha Trang.*

the beach, is another different Nha Trang – Nha Trang as Oriental fishing port. Take a stroll crossing the Hara Bridge over the **Cai River Bridge** early in the morning and there are plenty of photo opportunities as the red and blue **fishing boats** come in from the night's fishing. Jostling for mooring space between the **stilt houses** that line the banks, the fishermen paddle to shore in their extraordinary round *thung chai* basket boats.

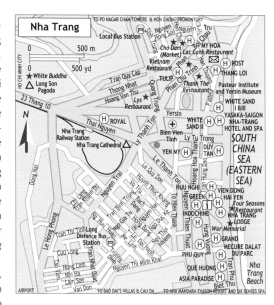

Beside the **Hara Bridge**, Nha Trang has its own rather impressive Cham **monuments**, where a steady stream of worshippers bearing offerings impart a very real sense of religious devotion.

NHA TRANG SIGHTS
Po Nagar Cham Towers

Known locally as **Thap Ba** (Lady of the City), these red brick towers, built between the 7th and 12th centuries, rise above the far bank of the Cai River, attractively sited on a flat hilltop overlooking the bridge and fishing harbour at the mouth of the river. Although the site has been used for Hindu worship since the 2nd century, the two principal towers honour the **Goddess of Po Nagar**, goddess of the Dua Liu clan, who ruled the southern region of the Cham Kingdom. The earliest wooden tower built on the site was burnt by the Javanese in AD774 and replaced by a brick and stone tower in AD784, the first of its kind. Of the original seven or eight towers, only four remain. The north tower, Thap Chinh, 23m (75ft) high, was built in AD817. Inside is a black stone statue of the goddess Uma. The central tower, Thap Nam, built in the

MY LAI MASSACRE

The most infamous US atrocity during the Vietnam War was committed on the morning of 16 March 1968, when US Army infantry units were sent on a search-and-destroy mission 13km (8 miles) from Quang Ngai City. The city includes Son My subdistrict, comprising four hamlets of which My Lai was one. Although meeting no resistance, the US soldiers immediately started killing unarmed men, women and children. In all, 504 people were slaughtered, most at My Lai. Today, the dead are commemorated by a memorial, a few graves and a small museum.

12th century, holds a stone *linga* (a phallic symbol of male creation and Siva). The south tower, Mieu Dong Ham, also houses a *linga*. The northwest tower, Thap Tay Bac, was originally devoted to Ganesha, the Hindu god represented by an elephant. The thick pillars to the right of the steps leading to the complex had originally supported the roof of a *mandala*, a rest house for pilgrims. The towers are a splendid example of Cham **architecture**, but what is more fascinating is that the site is still venerated.

Hon Chong Promontory

Not far beyond Po Nagar and off to the right, this promontory is a local beauty spot offering superb coastal views. There is a beach, but a nearby village renders it unsuitable for swimming.

Below: *A Cham religious sanctuary at Nha Trang, honouring Mother Goddess Po Nagar who is said to have taught local people new agricultural techniques.*

Long Song Pagoda

Look up anywhere in town and chances are you will glimpse an enormous white Buddha. Just west of the railway station (on 23 Thang 10 Street) stands the much renovated 19th-century Long Song Pagoda. The pagoda, topped with flamboyant glass and ceramic roof-ridge decoration, still has resident monks. Dominating the town from a nearby hill looms the 9m (30ft) white seated **Buddha**, defiantly erected in 1963 to commemorate the monks and nuns who died by self-immolation protesting the rule of South Vietnamese president Ngo Dinh Diem.

Nha Trang Cathedral

Returning towards the town centre, 23 Thang 10 Street leads into Thai Nguyen Street, at the end of which is the **cathedral**. Built in the 1930s on a small rock outcrop, this single-towered neo-Gothic building has a certain presence. Masses take place daily.

Bao Dai's Villas

South of Nha Trang Beach, the land rises to a

promontory occupied by Bao Dai's Villas. Built in the 1920s for the emperor, these five villas were later used by high-ranking South Vietnamese officials as holiday homes, next by the newly powerful Northern government officials and today as tourist guesthouses. The stupendous view no doubt compensates for the mostly genuine period furnishings that would appeal to the highly romantic.

Cau Da

South of the headland is what used to be the muddy shore of a small fishing village, Cau Da. It has been developed as a modern quay serving a couple of dozen excursion boats waiting to take visitors to the islands. A new **aquarium** that defies credibility – the entrance to the ghostly Disney-like galleon that contains the aquarium is through the gargantuan mouth of a lion fish – has been built on a nearby island. At a fishing village on one of the islands, visitors are brought ashore in the tipsy round *thung chai* **basket boats**. One resort, Vinapearl, has been built on Tri Island, reachable by the unlikely means of a cable car. There is excellent snorkelling and scuba diving in the clear waters, of the surrounding bays offering an enormous variety of designer tropical **fish** and delicate waving, living **corals**.

Excursions from Nha Trang
Doc Let Beach

Some consider this beach to be the most spectacular in Vietnam, long and wide with powder-white sand and shallow water. There are few visitors except at weekends. It lies on a peninsula 30km (18 miles) north of Nha Trang, past photogenic salt fields.

Opposite: *Da Lat is the playground of Vietnamese honeymooners – there are boats to rent here.*

Buon Ma Thuot

Northwest of Nha Trang, 194km (116 miles) on a good – if steep – road, Buon Ma Thuot is the centre for visits to minority hill tribe villages (permits obtained from any local travel agency). The Ethnographic Museum – which used to be another of Bao Dai's villas – at the corner of Nguyen Du and Le Duan Streets is open from Monday to Saturday (07:30–11:00 and 14:00–17:00). It displays artefacts of the 31 ethnic groups in Dac Lac Province. This is a **coffee** plantation area and you can buy coffee to take home at Nguyen Coffee Sales near the corner of Hai Ba Trung and Ama Trang Long. The rainy season is between April and November.

Yok Don National Park

Yok Don National Park is Vietnam's largest national park. The approach is via Ban Don Village northwest from Buon Ma Thuot. The **M'nong**, a matrilineal tribe that lives in the area, hunt wild elephants using domesticated **elephants**. Elephant rides can be booked through local travel agencies in Buon Ma Thuot. In the park are some 70 species of animals, 38 listed as endangered in Indo-China and 17 of those, worldwide, plus 200 species of birds. Buses travel to Ban Don from Buon Ma Thuot (booked through local travel agents) 45km (27 miles) away, or 148km (89 miles) north from Da Lat.

Kon Tum

About 246km (147 miles) north of **Buon Ma Thuot**, and 436km (262 miles) away from Nha Trang, lies Kon Tum, an awkward place to get to. It involves at least one overnight, but *montagnard* neighbourhoods literally ring the fringes of Kon Tum, making it unnecessary to have a permit.

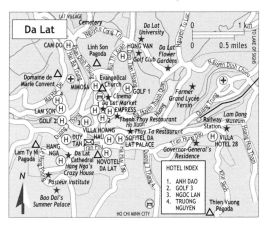

DA LAT

This Central Highlands hill resort lies 212km (132 miles) southwest of Nha Trang (or fly directly from Ho Chi Minh City, Danang or Hanoi – there are no flights from Nha Trang). The route heads first south along the coast down Highway 1 and then turns inland to Highway 11 at Phan Rang. Just off the road

near Phan Rang stand another couple of beautifully restored Cham towers. From here the road begins to climb the mountains in a series of startling switchbacks. At the highest point is **Ngoan Muc Pass** at 980m (3215ft), which the French called Bellevue Pass; the views are truly stunning, stretching out across the plain towards the coast.

Surviving the Vietnam War virtually unscathed, Da Lat remains today comparatively prosperous with a present population of about 189,000. On approaching the town, the villages seem neater, the children better dressed, and generally there is a feeling of greater spaciousness than what is found in the more densely populated lowlands.

Da Lat was created as a hill station in the early 20th century, following a visit to the area in 1897 by Dr Alexandre Yersin, the founder of the Pasteur Institute in Nha Trang. He thought the location, a hilly plateau at an elevation of 1475m (4839ft) above sea level, would make an ideal therapeutic retreat for Europeans suffering from the debilitating effects of lowland Vietnam's tropical climate.

The name Da Lat is a composite of two words: *da*, meaning 'water', and *Lat*, the name of a tribal people who have traditionally inhabited the region. The water of the lakes was an attraction for the French. The Lat were not and got shunted aside. By 1912, the hills surrounding the site's pleasant bowl-like depression

DA LAT RAILWAY

From the 1930s until it was closed in 1964 due to a series of guerrilla attacks, a cog railway linked Da Lat to the coast. Today, Da Lat Railway Station is one of the town's curious little sights. A few kilometres of track have been reopened and railway enthusiasts can enjoy a jaunt into the Da Lat suburbs aboard a Russian-built diesel.

DA LAT CLIMATE

Da Lat enjoys the unoriginal soubriquet 'City of Eternal Spring'. Throughout most of the year, days are bright and pleasantly warm and the nights cool, even cold in December and January. The rainy season is from May to November.

Above: *Da Lat's temperate climate encourages the cultivation of an abundance of exotic fruits and vegetables, which are artfully arranged on market stalls.*
Below: *The Central Highlands are home to a variety of ancient hilltribes – or* montagnards *– now struggling to maintain their unique way of life.*

had become dotted with European half-timbered villas that might have been lifted from Normandy to create a town that the French referred to affectionately, if incongruously, as 'Little Paris'.

With an average annual temperature of a very comfortable 18°C (65°F), the highland retreat earned a reputation as a salubrious spot. 'The pure bracing air stimulates the appetite', claimed a 1930s guidebook, 'and induces an inclination for physical exercise and brainwork, such as is never experienced at Saigon.' The area also had **agricultural** potential, and the temperate **climate** and fertile soil were suitable for cultivating a variety of cash crops such as vegetables, tea and coffee, and more recently grapes from which a very drinkable wine is now being produced. The strongest economic factor, however, is what it has always essentially been – **tourism** – and Da Lat is once again attracting thousands of Vietnamese tourists annually, especially honeymooners.

DA LAT SIGHTS

Perhaps because it was created as an escape, Da Lat draws much of its charm from an element of theatrical fantasy. The alpine woods, the neat villas, and a few veteran white Peugeot 203 taxis, all speak of elsewhere. Half the fun of sightseeing comes from simply wandering around the town's hillsides dotted with musty European-style villas and, like rummaging in someone's attic, marvelling at all the curious oddities.

For more specific sightseeing, Da Lat's focal point is **Xuan Huong Lake**, which lies in the southeastern part of the town. Created by damming the western end of the valley, the lake is quite pleasant with a couple of lakeside

restaurants. Paddle boats, some shaped like swans, are for hire. To the north are the **Da Lat Flower Gardens** with a robust display of orchids as well as temperate plants.

West of the lake's southern end and at the centre of the downtown area is the huge **Da Lat Market**. Built in the fifties, the main attractions are the stalls selling wood carvings, tribal baskets and weaving, tropical flowers and fruit, and a variety of teas.

Immediately northwest of Da Lat Market, continuing down the other side of the hill to Phan Dinh Phung Street, is an area for walking amid a townscape largely unchanged in appearance from the 1930s.

Da Lat Cathedral is located south of the town centre on Tran Phu Street near the Da Lat Palace Hotel. Built in the 1930s, this elegant building – with its single, shapely 47m (154ft) spire and French stained-glass windows – is a prominent landmark that sets historic Da Lat's quintessential Gallic tone.

Further religious landmarks are the **Domaine de Marie Convent**, now inhabited by a fraction of its once 300 nuns, easily recognizable for its tiled roofs and hilltop location on Ngo Quyen Street, and the pink-coloured **Evangelical Church** on Nguyen Van Troi Street.

Da Lat does not, for obvious reasons, boast venerable pagodas, although it has a few of interest. **Linh Son Pagoda**, on Phan Dinh Phung Street, about 1km (0.6 miles) north of the town centre, was founded in 1938 and is noted for its enormous bell, said to be cast of bronze and gold. **Quan Am Tu Pagoda** (Lam Ty Ni Pagoda), at 2 Thien My Street, is remarkable for one monk, Vien Thuc, who has worked tirelessly to develop the pagoda gardens; he is also a prolific painter. **Thien Vuong Pagoda**, sited on a pine-shaded hilltop on Khe Sanh Street about 4km (2.5 miles) southeast of town, is a Chinese temple known

> ### PO KLONG GARAI TOWERS
>
> Atop a small cactus-covered hill along the road to Da Lat, about 6km (4 miles) from Phan Rang, stands a group of four late 13th-century Cham towers. Purists may deplore their renovation, but silhouetted against the sky in their isolated location, they are impressive. An image of a dancing Siva can be seen over the main entrance to the biggest tower.

Below: *Beautiful orchids bloom in the Da Lat Flower Gardens.*

DA LAT GOLF COURSE

Back in the swing of things, Da Lat's golf course is situated on the north shore of Xuan Huong Lake. The place where Emperor Bao Dai knocked a few balls about in the 1940s and 1950s has recently been transformed into the smart 18-hole Pine Lake Golf Club. The club has great views and is open to all, but it is rather expensive.

for its three huge gilded sandalwood statues. These statues are the largest in Vietnam and the centre one represents Sakyamuni, the Buddha of the Past.

Two secular buildings not to be missed are **Bao Dai's Summer Palace** and the **Governor-General's Residence**. They are both open daily 07:00–11:00 and 13:30–16:30 (the latter closed when there is a conference). The former, set in attractive gardens about 2km (1.2 miles) southwest of the town centre on Le Hong Phong Street, is a big, airy 1930s villa complete with ornate throne and several portraits of the empress. The Governor-General's Residence, set on another hill, off Tran Hung Dao Street (the address of several large colonial villas) is of similar vintage and retains a certain stately air in its ambience (sometimes closed when in use for conferences).

AROUND DA LAT

The countryside around Da Lat is typified by pine-clad hills, rivers and waterfalls. Local beauty spots include the **Lake of Sighs** (Ho Than Tho), some 5km (3 miles) northeast of town, and the **Valley of Love**, 5km (3 miles) north of Da Lat. Both have boating facilities. For the more energetic, Lang Bian Mountain, about 12km (7.5 miles) to the northwest, offers a three- to four-hour hike up a five-peak mountain, which tops 2000m (6560ft) and affords wonderful views.

Below: *Golf has now been added to Vietnam's visitor attractions.*

Lat Villages

Of nine hamlets 12km (7 miles) north of Da Lat, five are inhabited by Lat ethnic people, the other three by Chill, Ma and Koho tribes, each speaking a different dialect. Lat houses are built on stilts and the villagers survive by growing rice, coffee, black beans and sweet potatoes. (More Lat villages around Buon Ma Thuot.)

Nha Trang and the Central Highlands at a Glance

October to **February** are the best months when it is dry and cool in the Central Highlands.

Vietnam Airlines serves Nha Trang from HCMC, Hanoi or Da Nang and Dalat (from HCMC only). A fast **train** links Nha Trang to HCMC, slow trains only from Da Nang or Hue. Or, it's a long **bus** ride from Hoi An or Phan Thiet (Mui Ne), arranged by tourist cafés.

In Da Lat and Nha Trang use taxis, *cyclos* and motorbike taxis, or rent a bike or motorbike from hotels and cafés. In hilly Da Lat it's metered taxis or motorbikes.

Nha Trang
LUXURY

Ana Mandara, Beachside Tran Phu Blvd, tel: 58 352 4705, reservations-nhatrang@six senses.com www.sixsenses. com/evason-anamandara Still one of the most charming luxury beach resorts in Vietnam. Carp pools, elegant cottages, thatched spa rooms on the beach surrounded by moats.
Sunrise Beach Resort, 12-14 Tran Phu St, tel: 58 382 0999, info@sunrisenhatrang.com.vn www.sunrisenhatrang.com.vn Newcomer on the promenade, this pricey five-star hotel offers all the luxury you might expect.

MID-RANGE

Nha Trang Lodge, 42 Tran Phu Street, tel: 58 352 1500, nt-lodge@dng.vnn.vn www.nhatranglodge.com Good value in this Malaysian-Vietnamese hotel.
Asia Paradise Hotel, 06 Biet Thu, tel: 58 352 4686, sales @asiaparadisehotel.com www.asiaparadisehotel.com Only a few steps from the beach, this new hotel with eccentric chartreuse furniture has a tiny rooftop pool. Good value.

BUDGET

Que Huong Hotel, 60 Tran Phu Boulevard, tel: 58 352 4686, khtourism@dng.vnn.vn www.quehuonghotel.com.vn This newish hotel on the promenade offers tasteful comfort: there's a sauna, a pool – even a tennis court. This hotel offers extremely good value.

Da Lat
LUXURY

Hotel Sofitel Da Lat Palace, 12 Tran Phu Street, tel: 63 382 5457, www.sofitel.com One of Asia's grand old hotels; very pricey.

Mercure Dalat du Parc, 7 Tran Phu Street, tel: 63 382 5777, Mercure.Reservations@ DalatResorts.com www. mercure.com Restored to modern comfort.

MID-RANGE

Empress Hotel, 5 Nguyen Thai Hoc Street, tel: 63 383 3888, empresdl@hcm.vnn.vn This tasteful villa-style hotel overlooks the lake. Excellent value and location.
Golf 3 Hotel, 4 Nguyen Thi Minh Khai Street, tel: 63 382 6042, golf3.dalat@vinagolf.vn www.vingagolf.vn This sleek hotel is the effort of the local tourist authority.

Nha Trang
Lac Canh Restaurant, 44 Nguyen Binh Khiem Street, tel: 58 382 1391. For 50 years this no-frills restaurant has been serving excellent seafood – try the marinated shrimp charcoaled at your table.

Nha Trang
Numerous dive shops organize trips to the islands.

NHA TRANG	J	F	M	A	M	J	J	A	S	O	N	D
AVERAGE TEMP. °F	75	77	79	81	83	83	82	82	82	79	77	76
AVERAGE TEMP. °C	23	25	26	27	28	28	28	28	28	26	25	23
RAINFALL in	2	1	2	2	2	2	2	2	7	13	15	7
RAINFALL mm	47	17	52	53	55	49	43	51	167	326	376	167
DAYS OF RAINFALL	10	4	4	5	8	8	8	9	15	18	18	18

6
Ho Chi Minh City (Saigon)

Travelling south in Vietnam effectively means following the migratory route of the Viets as they pushed the Chams further and further south. Today the Chams are still clustered around Phan Rang situated on the coast south of Nha Trang, with a thin sprinkling in the Mekong Delta.

At 300 years old, **Ho Chi Minh City** is relatively young as a Vietnamese metropolis. It received an influx of Chinese immigrants in 1778 and in 1978 the reverse took place – an exodus with the introduction of anti-Chinese policies by the Hanoi government, confiscating Chinese property and assets.

Prior to the arrival of the French, Ho Chi Minh City was a trading settlement with one wooden fort. The French took control of the city in 1859, making it the capital of their southern colony, **Cochinchina**. With the French came stylish government buildings, a cathedral, broad boulevards and elegant villas – and even an opera house and baguettes.

During the **American War**, foreign correspondents filled the hotels and Ho Chi Minh City became the R & R capital of Vietnam for American troops. Drinking bars had flourished as well as prostitution and the city developed a reputation for tawdry sleaze. When the Americans left, the free-wheeling, free-for-all pre-1975 city had to change. With the arrival of new government officials from the north and the renaming of the city in 1978, Ho Chi Minh City was forced to develop a new, slightly less tarnished image. Today, once again, it thrives as the Vietnamese city, most pro-western, modern, sophisticated, trendy, and

DON'T MISS

*** History Museum: explore this splendid collection from all periods.
*** Reunification Palace: gain insight into modern history at what was once the Presidential Palace.
*** Giac Lam Pagoda: visit Saigon's oldest temple.
** Cao Dai temple: witness an unbelievable baroque extravaganza at Tay Ninh.
*** Mui Ne: experience this delightful small beach resort.
** Cu Chi Tunnels: sense a haunting reminder of war.

Opposite: *The hustle and bustle of the market in cosmopolitan Ho Chi Minh City.*

Below: *River Saigon which lies to the east of the city.*

entrepreneurial – its wheeler-dealer, free-for-all spirit having been rapidly rejuvenated in the wake of the recent economic liberalization.

With an official population figure of 6.1 million, Ho Chi Minh City is Vietnam's largest city and a major port, located on the western bank of the Saigon River a few kilometres upstream from its outpouring into the South China Sea. The city is the nation's hub of revitalized commercial enterprise and exudes an almost palpable air of confidence from behind the renovated façades of hotels, new restaurants and bars. Hordes of shiny new motorbikes snarl the streets. Shops and markets are stocked with the latest imported technology, such as, televisions, videos and computers.

Geographically, Ho Chi Minh City is 1700km (1062 miles) from **Hanoi** but since the *doi moi* (open door) policy of 1988, encouraging foreign investment, the two cities have been drawing closer and closer together and competing for investment capital, be it Australian, Japanese, Korean, Taiwanese or American. In spite of all the upheaval of recent decades, little has changed in the city's original commercial aspirations.

Administratively, Ho Chi Minh City is divided into 12 urban districts (*quan*) and six suburban areas, although the main tourist facilities are mostly contained within the central District 1, lying between the river and Le Duan Boulevard and focused around the parallel streets of Nguyen Hue Boulevard and Dong Khoi Street. The other main area of interest is **Cholon**, the old **Chinatown**, located a few streets to the southwest. The riverside provides additional interest with small boats plying for trade near the major hotels.

CITY SIGHTS

Central Ho Chi Minh City is a fairly compact town and can be comfortably covered on foot, although, *cyclos* hired by the hour are always a pleasant way to travel, also providing an excellent view of the beautiful

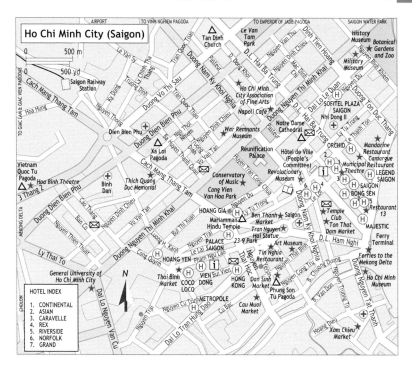

Ho Chi Minh City (Saigon)

HOTEL INDEX
1. CONTINENTAL
2. ASIAN
3. CARAVELLE
4. REX
5. RIVERSIDE
6. NORFOLK
7. GRAND

city. The circuit up Nguyen Hue Boulevard, along Le Loi Boulevard and down Dong Khoi Street makes a pleasant route, while on Sunday nights, it is the scene of the *chay rong rong* (literally, 'living fast'), an endless parade of hundreds of young people cruising on motorbikes, anxious to see and be seen.

Municipal Theatre ★

Located on Dong Khoi, near the Continental and Caravelle hotels, the theatre was built in 1900 and was originally intended as a French opera house, although it lacks the architectural grandeur of its Hanoi counterpart. Transformed into South Vietnam's National Assembly in 1955, it is now once again a theatre staging anything from traditional **Vietnamese theatre** to modern pop groups. Performances at 20:00.

GENTLE WARNING

Camera and bag snatching has become a real danger, even in daytime. Keep valuables in the hotel safe and wear only a covered safety belt with camera straps crossed over the chest. Be especially careful leaving clear-glass ATM booths. And do not wear expensive watches or jewellery in the street.

MUSEUMS

History Museum, on Nguyen Binh Khiem. A fine collection of prehistoric, Cham and ethnic artefacts illustrating the numerous cultures of Vietnam. Open from Tuesday to Sunday (08:00–11.30 and 13:00–16:30).

War Remnants Museum, formerly the Museum of Chinese and American War Crimes, corner of Le Qui Don and Vo Van Tan. Horrific insights into the Vietnamese point of view on the war (open 07:30–11:45 and 13:30–16:45).

Museum of Ho Chi Minh City, formerly the Museum of the Revolution, 27 Ly Tu Trong Street. Exhibits in the former residence of the French governor of Cochinchina illustrating the Communist struggle. Open from Tuesday to Sunday (08:00–16:00).

Ho Chi Minh Museum, 1 Nguyen Tat Thanh Street, once the offices of a shipping company where Ho signed on as a ship's cook and left Vietnam in 1911. Open daily (08:00–16:00).

Fine Arts Museum, 97A Pho Dun Chinh Street, classical to social realism exhibits. Open from Tuesday to Sunday (09:00–16.30).

Opposite: *East meets West – the Hotel de Ville provides a European backdrop to a typically Asian scene.*

Hotel de Ville ★★

At the northwestern end of Nguyen Hue Boulevard, what was the City Hall under the French now houses the Ho Chi Minh City's **People's Committee**. A sunny, yellow-and-white gothic parody of the Hotel de Ville in Paris, it was constructed in the first years of the 20th century and is remarkable for the incongruity of its ornate European **architecture** set in the middle of an Asian city. Probably the most photographed building in town, it stands across the street from a statue of **Ho Chi Minh** in a small park where old men play draughts (checkers).

Notre Dame Cathedral ★★

Standing in a square at the top of Dong Khoi Street is the red-brick, neo-Romanesque Catholic cathedral built by the French between 1877 and 1883. With imposing twin towers and an attractive interior, the entrance to **Notre Dame** is dominated by a statue of the **Virgin Mary** – its stained-glass windows were a casualty of World War II.

General Post Office ★

On the eastern side of the square stands the French-built post office dating from the 1880s. Its splendid colonial-style **architecture** somehow resembles a European railway station more than a post office.

Reunification Palace ★★★

Also known as the **Thong Nhat Conference Hall**. Situated on the south of the cathedral along Nguyen Du Street stands what was the **Presidential Palace** prior to 1975. In an image from a famous press photograph that came to symbolize the fall of Ho Chi Minh City (Saigon), a North Vietnamese tank crashes through the main gates of the Palace (30 April 1975). The original 19th-century building that occupied the site was the residence of the **French governor**. In 1962, two Vietnamese air force pilots bombed the building in a vain attempt to assassinate **President Diem**. The partially destroyed building was then pulled down and a new palace built. The exterior is typical of 1960s architecture, while inside are a conference hall, banquet hall and meeting rooms of stately proportions, the private apartments of the president and an underground operations centre.

War Remnants Museum *

It is close to the Reunification Palace, at 28 Vo Van Tan Street, and presents a largely photographic display (there is some hardware on show, ranging from a turn-of-the-century French guillotine to captured American weaponry) of man's **inhumanity** to man, predictably much of it US initiated during the war. Although grisly and sobering, it is a compelling **tourist attraction**. The museum is open daily (07:30–11:45 and 13:30–16:45).

History Museum ★★★

Open daily except on Mondays (08:00–11.30 and 13:00–16:00) and situated at the north end of Le Duan Boulevard, at Nguyen Binh Khiem Street, in the grounds of the **Botanical Gardens and Zoo**, this museum should not be missed. Housed in an imposing 1920s building of what could be called neo-Vietnamese architecture is a fine collection of **sculpture**, **pottery** and other artefacts from all major **historical periods**, from the Bronze Age Dong Son civilization through the Funan, Chenla, Khmer and Cham periods, the various minorities and Vietnamese dynastic eras.

TRAN HUNG DAO

Although Ho Chi Minh City wasn't on the map when Tran Hung Dao repelled a Mongol invasion in 1287, the national hero is well remembered in the city. A robust statue of a fearsome-looking Tran Hung Dao stands in Hero Square facing the river, while a temple dedicated to the general, at 34 Vo Thi Sau Street, has bas-reliefs depicting his exploits.

USEFUL CONTACTS

Hanoi Tourism: 72 Ton That Tung Street, District 1, tel: 8 3525 2843, saigon@ hanoitourist-travel.com
Saigon Tourist: 49 Le Thanh Ton, tel: 8 3827 9279, www.saigontourist.net
Vietnam Tourism: Room M1402, 225 Ben Chuong Duong, Go Gian Ward, District 1, tel: 8 3837 0788, info@vntourism.com

HO CHI MINH CITY PAGODAS

Ho Chi Minh City has far more pagodas than a brief visit could possibly encompass. Some of the best are in Cholon (see page 101). The following is a shortlist of the most striking:

Emperor of Jade (Ngoc Hoang) Pagoda ★★★

Dating from the turn of the century, this atmospheric pagoda, at 73 Mai Thi Luu Street, north of Dien Bien

Right: *Imposing temple architecture is softened by muted pink exteriors.*

Phu Street just before the Thi Nghe Channel, blends **Taoism** and **Buddhism** in its dedication to various Chinese and Vietnamese divinities – the Emperor of Jade is the supreme god of the Taoists. In addition to the temple's statuary and rich ornamentation, the **Hall of Ten Hells** is noted for its carved wooden panels depicting the torments that await the ungodly. **Prayers**, chanting with drums, bells and gongs, take place at 4:00 and 11:00 and 16:00 and 19:00.

Giac Lam Pagoda ★★★

Dating from 1774, this is probably Ho Chi Minh City's oldest pagoda. Located in the western part of the city in Tan Binh District at 118 Lac Long Quan Street, the pagoda is enormously appealing for its traditional architecture, decoration and numerous statues, funerary tablets and other religious artefacts. The compound holds a sacred *bodhi* tree from Sri Lanka.

Giac Vien Pagoda ★★★

In District 11 southwest of the city, next to Dam Sen Lake at 247 Lac Long Quan Street, Giac Vien is similar in style and atmosphere to Giac Lam Pagoda. Giac Vien's main attraction is its superbly carved **statues** of Buddha and other divinities.

Vinh Nghiem Pagoda ★★

At 339 Nam Ky Khoi Nghia Street in District 3 (north-west of the central area), this is a modern pagoda, completed in 1973 with aid from the Japan-Vietnam Friendship Association. It has the distinction of being Ho Chi Minh City's largest pagoda. The architectural style is Japanese influenced and the most dominant feature is a classic seven-storey tower with statues of the **Buddha** on every level. Two fierce warriors guard the pagoda entrance. Behind the large sanctuary is a three-storey funeral tower containing burial urns.

Xa Loi Pagoda ★

At 89 Ba Huyen Thanh Quan Street, near Dien Bien Phu Street in District 3 (northwest of Reunification Palace), Xa Loi Pagoda offers more **historical** than aesthetic interest. Built in 1956, the pagoda became a famous centre of protest against the regime of President Diem and in August 1963, it was violently **raided** by armed government forces. The incident served to consolidate Buddhist opposition to Diem and several monks committed self-immolation at the pagoda in protest. Of note among the pagoda buildings is a multi-tiered tower that enshrines a relic of the **Buddha**.

CHOLON

Comprising District 5, southwest of central Ho Chi Minh City, Cholon is the original **Chinese town**, built at the end of the 18th century. The name translates as 'Big Market' and the district, like Chinatowns elsewhere, is a commercial area, a hive of entrepreneurial activity with family businesses conducted from little shophouses packed cheek-by-jowl in bustling, narrow streets.

In spite of thousands of Chinese fleeing Vietnam as a result of the discriminatory government policies in the late seventies, Cholon retains its quintessential Chinese flavour. Highlights are the Chinese **pagodas**, whose tiled roofs and typically flamboyant decoration break the urban monotony. The following sights are within easy walking distance of one another.

> ## HO CHI MINH CITY SHOPPING
>
> Shopping in Ho Chi Minh City can be rewarding. The best buys are concentrated in the Dong Khoi Street area. Antique-cum-junk shops offer a few lucky finds, especially Chinese and Vietnamese ceramics, but check on export restrictions. Otherwise contemporary paintings are a good buy, as is silk, while lacquerware and inlaid mother-of-pearl boxes can be found almost anywhere.

Below: *Light and dark: inside Nghia An Hoi Quan Pagoda.*

Thien Hau Pagoda ★★★

This pagoda, at 710 Nguyen Trai Street, dates from the early 19th century and is Cholon's largest and one of its busiest pagodas. It is dedicated to Thien Hau, **Goddess of the Sea**, and in addition to its statuary and other usual religious furnishings, the pagoda is remarkable for the richly detailed ceramic **friezes** decorating the roof.

Nghia An Hoi Quan Pagoda ★★

At 678 Nguyen Trai Street, the temple is dedicated to legendary Chinese warrior Quan Cong, whose glass-encased statue is at the main altar flanked by those of his companions, General Chau Xuong (on the left) and the Mandarin Quan Binh. A gilded carved wooden boat hangs over the entrance and, to the left, huge figures of Quan Cong's horse and groom.

Quan Am Pagoda ★★★

Located at 12 Lao Tu Street, the early 19th-century Quan Am Pagoda is another excellent example of typical Chinese pagoda architecture and ornamentation with multiple **courtyards** and a profusion of variously dedicated **altars**. Note the ceramic tableaux used as roof decoration, the beautiful gilded and lacquered door panels and **statues** including figures of A-Pho, the Holy Mother, and Quan Am, Goddess of Mercy, by the main altar and to the left, Dia Tang Vuong Bo Tat, the King of Hell.

Tam Son Hoi Quan Pagoda ★★

At 118 Trieu Quang Phuc Street, childless mothers come to pray at this 19th-century pagoda dedicated to Me Sanh, the Goddess of Fertility. The pagoda also displays statues of General Quan Cong and his horse and Thien Hau, Goddess of the Sea.

Cha Tam Church ★

Lying west of the above-mentioned cluster of pagodas at the end of Tran Hung Dao Boulevard, is the church where **President Ngo Dinh Diem** and his brother were **arrested** and **assassinated** in the coup of November 1963.

DAY EXCURSIONS FROM HO CHI MINH CITY

Cu Chi Tunnels ★★

On the way to Tay Ninh some 35km (22 miles) northwest of Ho Chi Minh City, the tunnels are an amazing concept rather than an arresting sight. What visitors see today is a small, somewhat enlarged, section of a 200km (125 miles) network of inter-connected and multi-storey **underground passages** averaging 1.5m (5ft) high and 0.7m (2ft) wide, which served as a huge subterranean Viet Cong base. Here, literally under the feet of the **US forces** who had a base in Cu Chi district, were **Communist** command posts, field hospitals, weapons factories, classrooms and living quarters.

All hand dug, the tunnels were begun by the **Viet Minh** in the forties as part of the struggle against the **French**. The underground system was then renovated and extended by the Viet Cong in the sixties when the war with the USA escalated. Although the Americans eventually discovered the existence of the tunnels, they could never ultimately destroy them, in spite of employing a special volunteer force of 'tunnel rats'. The full story is related in the book, *The Tunnels of Cu Chi*, by Tom Mangold and John Penycate.

A 50m (164ft) section of the tunnels is open to visitors and even these enlarged passages can induce claustrophobia. The visitors' centre displays a wall map showing the full extent of the underground system and tour guides give a brief history of the tunnels and a description of the conditions endured here by the Viet Cong.

Tay Ninh ★★★

Lying close to the Cambodian border 96km (60 miles) northwest of Ho Chi Minh City, Tay Ninh is often combined with Cu Chi on a full-day excursion. The small

Above: *All roads in Ho Chi Minh City seem eventually to lead to a market. Starting out as a trading settlement, Ho Chi Minh City continues to place importance on material pursuits.*

> **TEMPLE ETIQUETTE**
>
> Visitors to the Cao Dai Temple at Tay Ninh should not enter the central portion of the nave, nor should they wander in and out during services. It is also disrespectful for visitors to leave before a service has ended. Services usually last about one hour.

Above: *The only sand dunes in Vietnam rise well back from the sea, north of Mui Ne.*

provincial town is famous as the site of the Great Temple of the Cao Dai religion, one of Vietnam's home-grown faiths.

Dating from the 1930s, this Cao Dai 'cathedral' (services daily at 06:00, 12:00, 18:00 and 00:00) and headquarters of the religion stands amid a well-ordered complex of administrative buildings, residences and a hospital of herbal medicine. There is no mistaking the Great Temple itself, a yellow-painted, twin-towered baroque extravaganza, part European church, part Vietnamese pagoda. Even more dazzling is the eye-catching multi-coloured interior, where dragon-entwined columns and other typically exuberant Oriental-style ornamentation, compounded by Cao Dai symbolism, have a kaleidoscopic effect. It is not to everyone's taste. Travel writer Norman Lewis, on a visit in 1950, thought the Great Temple 'must be the most outrageously vulgar building ever to have been erected with serious intent. It was a palace in candy from a coloured fantasy by Disney; an example of funfair architecture in extreme form'.

It can be truly overwhelming, but it is probably the single most unforgettable building in the whole of Vietnam. Services at the Great Temple are held daily at 06:00, noon, 18:00 and midnight. With priests dressed in bright red, blue or yellow robes, the ceremonies are colourful affairs. Visitors are allowed and unobtrusive photography is permitted.

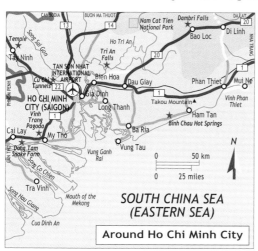

Around Ho Chi Minh City

Mui Ne Beach (Phan Thiet) ★★★

Vung Tau, which was previously known as **Cap St Jacques** by the French, may be the nearest beach to Ho Chi Minh City, but as it is on the delta near a refinery, it is not the most appealing. For powdery white sand and swaying palms, the nearest resort on the South China Sea is at **Phan Thiet** (the town), 200km (125 miles) from Ho Chi Minh City. The beach, **Mui Ne**, starts 11km (7 miles) further on. It is easily reached on a good road (Route 1 to Phan Thiet, then Route 706 to Mui Ne) in about four hours by car or bus through Ho Chi Minh City tourist cafés.

Mui Ne is a long stretch, 10km (6 miles) of white sandy beach along a peninsula, a fast-developing resort of budget to extremely luxurious hotels, all built since 1995. Many are air-conditioned bungalows scattered amongst tropical gardens around a pool, facing the sea, with a few of two or three storeys. One idiosyncrasy, basin taps often only have cold water, which is warm anyway.

The international hotel chains have yet to arrive (exceptions are Novotel and EEM) – in short, a new resort that has reached maturity remarkably quickly.

Apart from lazing on the beach or by the pool, a couple of Cham towers, some rather spectacular sand dunes just north of town, a floating village of fishermen and a village producing *nuoc mam* (Vietnam's all-purpose seasoning sauce made from fermented fish), may entice you out the hammock, briefly.

Approximately 40 minutes to the south, or 28km (17 miles), on top of **Takou Mountain**, lies Vietnam's largest reclining Buddha at 49m (159ft) long – at the end of a 90-minute climb.

Rainy months are July, August and September. High season is December and January. Around **Tet**, rooms can be very tightly booked, but it is a great place to drop off and sleep to the sound of the sea.

Below: *Mui Ne beach near Phan Thiet, east of Ho Chi Minh City.*

Ho Chi Minh City (Saigon) at a Glance

Ho Chi Minh City is most comfortable from **December** through **February**.

Ho Chi Minh City's airport, Tan Son Nhat, is a 30-minute taxi ride from the city; get a metered taxi. Once through arrival formalities, facilities include money exchange, post office and a tourism information desk. Ho Chi **Minh City Railway Station** is in District 3, about 2km (1.25 miles) from the city centre at 1 Nguyen Thong Street, tel: 8 823 0105. Tourist cafés (local tour operators) arrange buses or a car and driver to Mui Ne.

The romantic way of getting around HCMC is by *cyclo*, a trifle unnerving at first, but the vantage point really does offer an excellent view of the city (take taxis after dark). Otherwise, take metered taxis or motorbike taxis (*xe om*) who station themselves at corners. Cars with drivers are available through hotels and tour companies. Bicycles or motorbikes can be hired from budget hotels. Local buses are not recommended.

Ho Chi Minh City (Saigon)
Ho Chi Minh City has numerous international luxury hotels and hundreds in the mid- and budget range. Best rates are negotiated through an agent.

LUXURY
Hotel Majestic, 1 Dong Khoi St, tel: 8 3829 5517, majestic @majesticsaigon.com.vn www.majesticsaigon.com.vn The only traditional hotel on the Saigon River, now renovated to five-star standard.
Caravelle Hotel, 19 Lam Son Square, District 1, tel: 8 3823 4999, hotel@caravellehotel. vnn.vn www.caravellehotel. com This renovated colonial hostelry opposite the Opera House has a pool and a nostalgic rooftop bar.
Legend Hotel Saigon, 2-4A Ton Duc Thang, tel: 8 3823 3333, info@legendsaigon.com www.legendsaigon.com Life-sized bronze horses and a fountain set the style of this riverside tower.
Equatorial Hotel, 242 Tran Binh Trong Street, Dist 5, tel: 8 3839 7777, info@equatorial. com www.equatorial.com/ hcm/ Host to numerous heads of state – and a seafood restaurant boasting every live shellfish in Vietnam. A real culinary treat!

MID-RANGE
Rex Hotel, 141 Nguyen Hue Blvd, District 1, tel: 8 3829 2185, rexhotel@rex.com.vn www.rexhotelvietnam.com Indochine nostalgia, a long established hotel (full of cane and rattan), with a kitch bar.
Continental, 132 Dong Khoi Street, tel: 8 3829 9201, continentalhotel@vnn.vn www.continentalvietnam.com Good enough for Graham

Greene and Jacques Chirac, beautifully renovated colonial style. Central, but no pool.
Grand Hotel, 8 Dong Khoi, District 1, tel: 8 3823 0163, grand-hotel@fmail.vnn.vn www.grandhotelsaigon.vn The beautifully renovated 1930s wing is dearer than the new.

BUDGET
Kim Long Hotel, 58 Mac Thi Buoi Street, District 1, tel: 8 3822 8558, kimlonghotel@ hcm.vnn.vn www.kimlong hotel.com Deluxe rooms in this centrally located minihotel with lift, have balconies, tubs with showers, AC and cable TV. Free internet.
Dong Do Hotel, 35 Mac Thi Buoi Street, District 1, tel: 8 3827 3637, info@dongdohotel. com www.dongdohotel.com Another new mini-hotel on 'budget street'. Lift, safes, some tubs with showers, cable TV.

Mui Ne beach (Phan Thiet)
All hotels listed have thatched pavilion restaurants.

LUXURY
Seahorse Resort and Spa, tel: 62 384 7507, info@seahorse resortvn.com www.seahorse resortvn.com This five-star, elegant newcomer, very central, has showers open to the sky. Competitively priced.
Victoria Phan Thiet Resort, Km 9 Phu Hai, tel: 62 381 3000, resa.phanthiet@ victoriahotels-asia.com

Ho Chi Minh City (Saigon) at a Glance

www.victoriahotels-asia.com
Rustic-style luxury bungalows
in bougainvillaea-draped
gardens by the sea.
**Novotel Ocean Dunes & Golf
Resort**, 1 Ton Duc Thang
Street, Phan Thiet, tel: 62 382
2393, novotel.reservations@
phanthietresorts.com www.
novotel.com/2067 Pricey
four-star resort; Nick Faldo
designed the golf course.

MID-RANGE
Coco Beach Resort, 58
Nguyen Dinh Chieu, tel: 62
384 7111/2/3, paradise@
cocobeach.net www.coco
beach.net French-German
owned, wooden bungalows
in tropical gardens on the
beach. Restaurant serving
French cuisine.
Full Moon Beach Resort, 84
Nguyen Dinh Chieu, Ham
Tien, tel: 62 384 7008, full
moon@windsurf-vietnam.com
www.windsurf-vietnam.com
Stone cottages with four-poster
beds, stylish furnishings, pool,
cable TV, some showers open
to the sky.

BUDGET
Sunrise Resort, 72 Nguyen
Dinh Chieu, tel: 62 384 7015,
pq@sunriseresort.com.vn
www.sunriseresort.com.vn
These relatively new, well-
designed rooms with terraces
are rare at the price. Cable
TV, telephones and a pool.
Best budget value.
SunShine Beach, 82 Nguyen
Dinh Chieu, tel: 62 384 7788,
info@sunshine-beach.com

www.sunshine-beach.com
Big glass windows with
French blinds and wrought-
iron beds lend this budget
hotel a bit of style. No pool,
but great value.
Hiep Hoa Resort,
80 Nguyen Dinh Chieu,
tel: 62 384 7262,
hiephoatourism@yahoo.com
www.muinebeach.net/hiep
hoa These simply furnished
two-storey blocks, some with
sea views, offer great value
for sacrificing a pool.

WHERE TO EAT

Mandarin, 11A Ngo Van
Nam, District 1, tel: 8 3822
9783. The locals consider
this the best, albeit pricey,
Vietnamese food.
Indochine Saigon, 32 Pham
Ngoc Thach, District 3, tel:
8 3823 9256. Gourmet
Vietnamese food in elegant
colonial villa and garden.
Hoi An, 11 Le Thanh Ton,
District 1, tel: 8 3823 7694.
This restaurant serves elegant
Vietnamese-style food.
The Temple Club, 29 Ton
That Thiep Street, District 1,
tel: 8 3829 9244. Here you
can enjoy good Vietnamese
food in clubby 1930s style
sitting room.

Augustin, 10 Nguyen Thiep
Street, tel: 8 3829 2941.
Serves inexpensive bistro-
type food.
Huong Lai, 38 Ly Tu Trong,
tel: 8 3822 6814. Excellent
Vietnamese food served by
former street children being
taught a trade.
Sesame, 157 Xo Viet Nghe
Tinh, Binh Thanh District, tel:
8 3899 3378. A hospitality
training school for orphans.

TOURS AND EXCURSIONS

Day tours are well developed
in HCMC, most private tour
operators and cafés are
cheaper than the pioneer,
state-run Saigon Tourist.
Vidotour, 145 Nam Ky Khoi
Nghia Street, District 3,
tel: 8 3933 0457,
info@vidotourtravel.com
www.vidotourtravel.com
Sinh Cafe, 127 Pho Ban Co,
Distric 3, tel: 8 333 4083,
pacifictravel@hn.vnn.vn
www.vietnamopentour.com

USEFUL CONTACTS

**HCMC Family Medical &
Dental Practice**, Diamond
Plaza, 34 Le Duan Street,
District 1, 24-hour tel: 8 3822
7848, lucy@vietnammedical
practice.com

HO CHI MINH CITY	J	F	M	A	M	J	J	A	S	O	N	D
AVERAGE TEMP. °F	78	80	83	85	83	82	80	80	81	80	79	79
AVERAGE TEMP. °C	26	27	28	29	28	28	27	27	27	27	26	26
RAINFALL in	0	0	0	2	9	12	12	11	13	10	5	2
RAINFALL mm	14	4	10	50	218	312	293	270	327	266	117	48
DAYS OF RAINFALL	2	1	2	5	18	22	23	22	23	21	12	7

7
The Mekong Delta and Phu Quoc Island

One would never imagine, standing in the midst of Ho Chi Minh City's snarling traffic, that hardly an hour away from this burgeoning metropolis is the intensely rural **Mekong Delta**, a green, watery realm that is quintessentially Vietnamese. The vast flatlands of this liquid maze make up Vietnam's 'rice bowl', and the towns of the delta act as little more than service stations to a rather sprawled patchwork of rice paddies criss-crossed by rivers, streams and canals.

Roads connecting the principal towns are surprisingly good and, seemingly, constantly being improved – the $35m **Friendship Bridge** between Ha Tien and My Tho, a joint venture between Australia and Vietnam, eliminates a time-consuming ferry. Hotel accommodation has improved in the last few years and now there are very comfortable air-conditioned rooms with hot water in all the cities, as well as in the recent arrival on the tourist map, Phu Quoc Island, off shore in the Gulf of Thailand. There are no major tourist sights in the delta and nor do the cities hold much appeal. Rather it is the delta itself and the people who live in this watery environment that fascinate the visitor.

Exploring the Mekong Delta
Covering slightly more than 3.7 million ha (9 million acres), from the air the delta looks like a great green carpet interlaced by the silvery threads of countless streams and canals. Thrusting through the green are the thick brown fingers of the **Mekong** and its tributary, the **Bassac** (known in Vietnamese, respectively, as the Tien and the Hau, the 'upper' and 'lower' rivers), which flow roughly 200km (125

Don't Miss

*** My Tho: a delightful delta port within easy reach of Ho Chi Minh City.
*** Can Tho: explore the unofficial delta capital with its own lively floating market.
*** Chau Doc: an attractive commercial centre with numerous floating houses.
*** Phu Quoc Island: laze on some of Vietnam's finest sandy beaches.
** Sam Mount: witness a rare elevation near Chau Doc covered with an assortment of religious buildings.

Opposite: *On the waterfront – a typical delta home, raised on stilts to offset the risk of flooding.*

LEGEND OF FUNAN

The Kingdom of Funan, the earliest civilization to occupy the Mekong Delta, rose to power through a successful blend of local culture and Indian influence. Long ago, so legend has it, there was a waterlogged land wherein lived a princess, the daughter of a naga king. One day a young Brahman named Kaundinya appeared at the shore. The princess went to greet the stranger and as she approached he shot an arrow from a magic bow into her boat. Frightened, she surrendered herself to him. They were married and Kaundinya became master of the watery realm. As a dowry, the naga king drank up the water that covered the country so that his new son-in-law might cultivate the soil.

miles) from Vietnam's border with Cambodia to the South China Sea (known in Vietnam as the Eastern Sea). Estuary islands further divide the mainstreams that then fan out in a classic delta pattern, finally flowing into the sea from eight mouths. But eight is an unlucky number, so the Vietnamese count one more small channel, thus giving the river its local name, **Cuu Long Giang** – meaning River of Nine Dragons.

Transforming the land between the streams into a watery maze is an intricate web of **canals**, some short and narrow, others long, wide highways – running as straight as a die 50km (30 miles) – and more to link the Bassac with the **Gulf of Thailand**. No one knows exactly the combined length of these waterways, although estimates put it close to 5000km (3125 miles) – nearly 1000km (625 miles) longer than the entire course of the Mekong River.

Ranging over nine administrative provinces, the Mekong Delta is flat – any spot above 5m (16ft) is quite rare – but it is not featureless. Topographical diversity is found in the **Plain of Reeds**, an extensive low-lying area in the north where 'floating' rice copes with the swampy conditions, and in the **U-Minh forest** on the Ca Mau peninsula to the south.

Wrested from the Khmer only in the 18th century, the Mekong Delta is the newest part of Vietnam. It is nonetheless of vital importance as the country's single largest tract of arable land. Today, 45 per cent of

Vietnam's total **rice** output comes from the delta. Also cultivated in significant quantities are **soya beans**, **maize**, **sorghum**, **peanuts**, **pineapples**, **sugar cane** and **coconut palms**, as well as **orchard fruits**.

The delta's calm, bucolic appearance belies what has at times been a rather violent past. From the days of the Nguyen lords, it was an area of **con-**

Left: *Characterized by its flatness, any elevation is unusual in the delta region.*
Opposite: *The Mekong Delta is laced in a network of canals dug to expand rice cultivation. A milder climate for the crop than in the Red River Delta enables the region to produce three crops annually.*

quest, **settlement**, and later resettlement as populations were shifted in the periodic upheavals of Vietnam's turbulent history. This factor, combined with the delta's economic significance, made the region, somewhat frequently, a hotbed of social **unrest**, fuelled by the iniquities of oppressive landlords. Here were warlords, river pirates and, lastly, communist insurgents.

During the **Vietnam War** the swampy flatlands were a stronghold of the Viet Cong and the area saw some of the most vicious fighting under the worst possible physical conditions. To quote an article published in *National Geographic* in 1968, 'War on any battlefield is a nightmare. The Mekong Delta compounds the horror. To fight here means tortuous slogging through snake-ridden swamps, where sucking mud grips the legs like wet concrete. The enemy may be only five feet away, yet unseen in the thick jungle.'

Today, with the fertile delta once again flourishing, it is hard to believe that modern warfare once turned this placid countryside into a nightmare.

Although overwhelmingly **rural**, the Mekong Delta does have several large **towns** – Can Tho has

CLIMATE

Between January and March the temperature in the Mekong Delta ranges between 22°C and 34°C (72°F and 93°F). The humidity and rainfall increase from May onwards, and the wettest months are between July and October. During this time, flooding may occur, which can restrict travel.

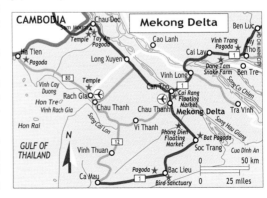

Above: *Ploughing fields the traditional way near My Tho.*

a population of 330,000, Long Xuyen 240,000, My Tho 180,000, and Vinh Long 124,000. These and other less important centres are sited along the main river channels, most often where intersected by major transportation canals. **Rach Gia**, (with a population of 180,000) on the Gulf of Thailand, is the only significant town on the sea coast.

The homogeneity of the delta – the population is overwhelmingly Vietnamese with a sprinkling of Khmer Krom (southern Khmer), Chinese and Cham – is contrasted by an amazing diversity of religious practice. Encountered within surprising proximity are more places of worship of different persuasion than perhaps any other rural area in the world – **Buddhist** temples of both the Theravada and Mahayana persuasions, **Catholic** churches, **Muslim** mosques, **Cao Dai** temples and **Chinese** shrines to various minor deities all add fascination to the charm of the surroundings.

Apart from the rural landscape and the region's religious mosaic, the other attraction of travelling through the delta is the early morning floating **markets**, typically held at the junction of two or more main canals.

To minimize the cost of boats, the easy way to explore the Delta is via the well-organized **tours** from Ho Chi Minh City. A wide variety are on offer from a one-day taster tour to My Tho, to three- or four-day tours around Can Tho and Chau Doc, and others that go up-river from Chau Doc to Phnom Penh.

MY THO

The closest Mekong town to Ho Chi Minh City and one of the most charming of the delta ports, **My Tho** lies 70km (45 miles) southwest of the metropolis in an area noted for its **rice paddies** and **fruit orchards**. The capital of Tien Gian Province, the town lies at a right angle formed by the

A REGION OF PLENTY

The French first saw the productive potential of the Mekong Delta region. They encouraged mass settlement of the area which was covered by forest until the late 19th century. Today, the region appears to have recovered from the ravages of the Vietnam War. Its markets are abundantly supplied with fish and a variety of fruits, vegetables and grains yielded by its rich alluvial soil.

junction of the Bao Dinh Channel and the northernmost branch of the Mekong. One of My Tho's greatest pleasures is simply to while away an hour or two in a café watching the **aquatic** world slip by or, better still, join it on a boat tour.

The narrow canals around My Tho are crossed by tiny wooden and bamboo bridges. The banks are fringed by water palms whose graceful fronds form green arches. These narrow canals are some of the most beautiful in the entire delta. Only five minutes away, **Tan Long** is a pretty little island, famous for its **longan orchards** (longans are related to lychees). **Phung Island**, about 20 minutes by boat, once held the open-air sanctuary of a small religious sect headed by the 'Coconut Monk'. Reputedly, monks were allowed nine wives, adding considerably to its attraction as a religion. Now visitors are shown a coconut candy 'factory'.

Tourist sights in My Tho include **Vinh Trang Pagoda**, a short distance from the town centre at 60A Nguyen Trung Truc Street, a delightful 19th-century pagoda with a wooden interior concealed behind a colonial façade added in 1907. **My Tho's Central Market**, a length of market stalls strung along Trung Truc and Nguyen Hue Streets, presents a lively, local scene. **My Tho Catholic Church**, located on the corner of Hung Vuong Boulevard

---

ISLAND OF THE COCONUT MONK

About 3km (2 miles) from My Tho, **Phung Island** was established as a retreat by the 'Coconut Monk' at the end of World War II. Ong Dao Dua, a charismatic leader, initiated a new religion that fused Buddhist and Christian elements. For three years he is said to have sat and meditated on a stone slab, sustained only by a diet of coconuts (hence the nickname). His philosophy advocated peaceful reunification of the country, for which he suffered persecution both by the South Vietnamese government and subsequently the communists.

Left: *A fisherman's houseboat: to the people of the Mekong Delta, the river provides both a living and a home. Fishing and rice-growing are the main economic activities of the region, although tourism is becoming increasingly popular.*

U-MINH FOREST

The world's largest mangrove swamp outside the Amazon covers some 1000km² (386 sq miles) of the Ca Mau peninsula, Vietnam's southernmost tip comprising the Mekong Delta province of Minh Hai. The area is well off the tourist track, although the town of Ca Mau, 179km (112 miles) southwest of Can Tho, provides basic facilities. U-Minh suffered severe damage from chemical defoliants during the Vietnam War and in spite of some recovery, remains under threat from local encroachment. An intriguing area for the naturalist or conservationist.

and Nguyen Trai Street, is a pleasant yellow-washed church dating from the late 19th century, serving a sizeable Catholic population.

VINH LONG

Capital of the province of the same name, **Vinh Long** is situated on the Mekong River some 65km (40 miles) southwest of My Tho. The town is little more than a pit-stop on the journey between My Tho and Can Tho; **boats** can be hired here for **excursions**. One possible excursion is by narrow wooden boat poled along metre-wide canals to **Xeo Quit**, a former Viet Cong base somewhat buried in the rainforest of **malucca** trees. It is now so still, the only sound to be heard is birdsong.

CAN THO

The fourth largest town in southern Vietnam and the unofficial capital of the delta, **Can Tho** is a university town as well as the biggest port on the Mekong River system. Situated 34km (21 miles) southwest of Vinh Long and 110km (69 miles) from the sea, Can Tho stands on the right bank of the Bassac at a point where the river is nearly 2km (1.2 miles) wide. The port receives ships of up to 5000 tons and there are plans to expand handling capacity from the present 150,000 tons a year. The **river** is Can Tho's principal feature; the town's only truly memorable sight is the lively and colourful **floating market** held at the junction of seven canals.

A typical boat excursion includes the floating market where huge **wooden boats**, wholesalers loaded

with mounds of cucumbers, water melons, flowers, onions, green beans, cabbages, star fruits, turnips and coconuts, sell to individuals in tiny slivers of boats that weave their way precariously in between. Typically, tours stop at a riverside **rice noodle factory** and a **rice mill** before weaving through rural canals lined with thatched shacks where children dance up and down, waving to get attention.

Alternatively, it can be pleasant simply to stroll along the new riverside promenade and around the town. Among the few landmarks is **Munirangsyaram Pagoda** at 36 Hoa Binh Boulevard. Built just after the war, it is a good example of the Theravada Buddhist pagodas that serve the delta's Khmer minority. **Can Tho Market** is a colourful, bustling affair paralleling the river along Hai Ba Trung Street.

LONG XUYEN

Some 62km (39 miles) up the Bassac from Can Tho is **Long Xuyen**, the capital of **An Giang Province**. Once the centre of the Hoa Hao religious sect, this spacious riverside town today seems somewhat wrapped up in a smug preoccupation with its reviving commercial prosperity. The one inescapable sight is an imposing, modern **Catholic church**. Perhaps of greater interest is the extremely lively and colourful **My Long Market**, located in Long Xuyen 2nd Centre and stocked by boats ferrying fresh produce across the river from the renowned fruit orchards of **Cho Moi District**.

Above: *Tropical forest cover in the Mekong Delta was once more extensive. Although much was destroyed during the Vietnam War when the delta provided a refuge for the Viet Cong, dense secondary rainforests have returned.*

Opposite: *Goods for sale in the shade of a colourfully decorated porticoed shopfront.*

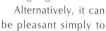

From Long Xuyen two directions can be taken; northwest up the Bassac to Chau Doc, or southwest to Rach Gia on the coast.

CHAU DOC

Chau Doc is the last town on the Bassac before the Cambodian border 55km (34 miles) from Long Xuyen. It is a small but prosperous **commercial centre**, attractively strung out along the right bank of the **Bassac**. In town there is a charming little blue-painted **Catholic church** built in 1920. Boat excursions from here pass a village of 2000 **floating houses** and **fish farms** – many Cambodian refugees fled here during the Khmer Rouge atrocities – to a **Cham village** across the river. There is a Muslim community centred around Chau Giang Mosque – there are no burkas here, only a few pillbox hats worn by young boys. The people speak Cham, their children study in Vietnamese at school and read the Koran in Arabic.

Particularly for Vietnamese tourists, the main attraction in this area is **Sam Mount**, about 3km (2 miles) southwest of Chau Doc. At the foot of the hill stands **Tay An Pagoda**, instantly recognized by its wildly colourful decoration. It enshrines a noted collection of some 200 wooden **religious statues**. Opposite is the **Temple of Lady Chua Xu** (Mieu Ba Chua Xu). The statue of the temple's namesake originally stood atop **Sam Mount** but was brought down in the early 19th century to be enshrined, first in a bamboo shelter and then in the present multi-roofed pagoda built in 1972. The temple's interior, sweet-smelling and heady with incense smoke, may be garish, though impressive for its crowds of suppliants who come to honour the holy lady and pray for good fortune before her statue. After Sam Mountain, tours stop at **Binh Duc**, a village engaged in making joss (incense) sticks from bamboo, sawdust, glue and a special ingredient that provides the scent. Daily production: 5000 for the workshop of three; individual pay: $2.

KHMER INFLUENCE

Until the middle of the 18th century, Chau Doc was part of Cambodia, and the area still supports a substantial Khmer population. Cambodia's influence is visible in the darker skin of its inhabitants and in the women's sartorial style, favouring scarves over the traditional *non la* conical hat. Chau Doc is also the seat of the Hoa Hao religion, which was founded in the nearby village of the same name in 1939.

RACH GIA

Facing the Gulf of Thailand, some 50km (30 miles) south-west of Long Xuyen, **Rach Gia** is the capital of Kien Giang Province and the delta's only significant coastal port. The town stands at the mouth of the **Cai Lon River** (the downtown area is actually an island formed by two branches of the river), and derives traditional prosperity from **fishing** and **rice cultivation**. There are a surprising number of **temples** and **pagodas**.

Phat Lon is a large 200-year-old Theravada Buddhist pagoda off Quang Trung Street on the north side of town. Also worth visiting, a short distance south at 18 Nguyen Cong Tru Street, is **Nguyen Trung Truc Temple**, dedicated to the 19th-century Vietnamese resistance fighter of the same name, executed by the French at the market place on 27 October 1868. In the centre of town, **Ong Bac De Pagoda** at 14 Nguyen Du Street is a 100-year-old pagoda that was built by the local Chinese community to honour Ong Bac De, the reincarnation of the Jade Emperor of Heaven, whose imposing statue stands in the main altar.

Secular sights include a small museum at 21 Nguyen Van Troi Street, and the bustling market located at the northeast end of the island.

RACH GIA SPECIALITIES

Rach Gia is noted for its seafood and has a comparatively good selection of restaurants serving both Chinese and Vietnamese food. Other delicacies to try include cuttlefish, eel, frogs' legs, turtle and, for the less squeamish, snake.

Opposite: *The delta's rich assortment of tropical fruit provides welcome refreshment.* **Left:** *The symmetry, light and colour characteristic of a Cao Dai temple interior.*

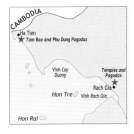

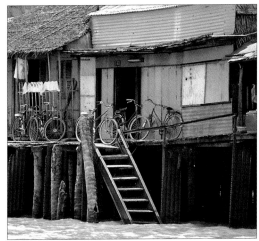

Right: *Stilt dwellings of the Mekong Delta. Bicycles and motorbikes provide the main land transport, though there are many more waterways than roads.*

HA TIEN

Situated a little over 90km (56 miles) north of Rach Gia and just 6km (4 miles) from the Cambodian border, the charming little coastal town of **Ha Tien** was part of the Khmer Kingdom until the early 18th century. It is noted for a couple of 18th-century pagodas – **Tam Bao Pagoda** and **Phu Dung Pagoda** – and for its scenic setting, including nearby **beaches**. A historic town subject to perennial invasions, lastly by the Khmer Rouge in the late 1970s, Ha Tien lives on in one of the little lost corners of the world.

PHU QUOC ISLAND

Only 15km (9 miles) south of the Cambodian border, 45km (28 miles) west of Ha Tien and 120km (74.5 miles) northwest of the port of Rach Gia, the elongated triangular island of **Phu Quoc**, population 85,000, has sprung on the tourism scene with the opening of several new **luxury resorts**, not surprisingly, as the island is bordered by some of the finest sandy beaches in Vietnam.

Part of a 22-island archipelago, unlike the Delta, Phu Quoc is **mountainous** and covered by a tangle of green jungle. In 2001, 70 per cent of the island, 31,422ha (77,644 acres), was declared a protected National Park.

Not a rice-producing area, the main crop here is black pepper and the islanders are fishermen. The island is best known in Vietnam for its high quality fermented fish sauce (*nuoc mam*) and its rather curious hunting dogs with ridged backs, curly tails and bluish tongues.

Phu Quoc has played an important role in Vietnam's history. It was to the island that Nguyen Anh, later Emperor Gia Long, scion of the Nguyen family of Hue, fled after his family's defeat in the Tay Son Rebellion. Here, he made history-turning contact with the French priest, Pigneau de Behaine in the 1760s and 1770s, who arranged French military support in establishing the Nguyen court in Hue. Phu Quoc was also known for its notorious Cay Dua (Coconut Tree) Prison, built by the French, later used by the Americans to hold 40,000 Viet Cong prisoners. Still used, the prison is now a national historic relic, complete with commemorative monument.

Apart from trekking and lazing by the beach, the island offers fishing, snorkeling and diving among the islands off to the south. The main town of Duong Dong, on the west coast, is not much of a town, the main sights being a kind of temple lighthouse, Dinh Cau, built in honour of Thien Hau, Goddess of the Sea, and the fish sauce factory – you'll smell it before you get there – not far from the market. The airport is almost within walking distance of town.

The port, An Thoi, is at the south extremity of the island and it is here that boats, fast and slow ferries, arrive and depart for Rach Gia.

Beaches virtually ring the island, but the most developed is Long Beach (Bai Cua Can), stretching almost 20km (12 miles) along the west coast from Duong Dong almost to An Thoi where the resorts have sprung up. On the southeast tip of the island, Bai Sao and Bai Dam are beautiful undeveloped beaches as well as Bai Khem, a military area closed to the public. Two more beaches, Bai Dai in the northwest and Bai Thom in the northeast, both lie in military zones (Phu Quoc is contested with Cambodia), but Bai Dai is open to the public and Bai Thom is open on Sundays. You need a motorbike over red dusty roads to get to them, until buses and taxis are introduced.

Oc-Eo

Located about 10km (6 miles) inland from Rach Gia, the remains of the city of Oc-Eo, dating from the 1st to the 6th centuries AD, is the most significant archaeological site relating to the ancient Kingdom of Funan. An important trade centre, Oc-Eo has yielded finds, including Roman coins, suggestive of the scope of Funan's contacts. There are also traces of the elaborate canal systems by which Funan was able to exert material supremacy in the delta. Archaeological importance, however, is not reflected in any tourist sights and Oc-Eo has little to offer the casual visitor.

The Mekong Delta and Phu Quoc Island at a Glance

BEST TIMES TO VISIT

Dec–Mar, when the weather is dry, warm and less humid.

GETTING THERE

The best hassle-free way to see the Delta is via **bus-and-boat tours** along the rivers and canals arranged by tourist cafés or travel agents in HCMC. Travelling independently, frequent air-conditioned **mini-buses** on good roads link HCMC, My Tho, Long Xuyen, Chau Doc Rach Gia and Can Tho. Or rent a **car** and **driver** through HCMC travel agents. For long-distance boats, check current schedules with HCMC travel cafés. (*See* excursions Chapter 6.)

GETTING AROUND

In towns by taxi, *cyclo*, motor-bike taxi or *xe loi* – motorbikes with a passenger cart.

WHERE TO STAY

LUXURY
Can Tho
Victoria Can Tho Hotel, Cai Khe Ward, tel: 71 381 0111, resa.cantho@victoriahotels-asia.com www.victoria hotels-asia.com A delightful riverside neo-colonial with atmosphere.

Chau Doc
Victoria Chau Doc Hotel, 1 Le Loi Street, tel: 76 386 5010, resa.chaudoc@victoriahotels-asia.com www.victoriahotels-asia.com Luxurious neo-Victorian grandeur, exquisite food; overlooks river.

Phu Quoc Island
Hotels are strung out south of town along the beach. All have restaurants, sometimes two.
Long Beach's Ancient Village, Cua Lap, To Village, tel: 77 398 1818, info@longbeachvn. com www.longbeachvn.cm In the tropical gardens of this newest luxury resort are temples, a covered bridge built without nails, canals and carp pools. Luxurious, antique-style rooms.
La Veranda, Ward, 1 Duong Dong Beach, Tran Hung Dao Street, tel: 77 398 2988, contact@laverandaresort.com www.accorhotels.com Novotel's delight neo-colonial resort is a play on a Thirties Indochine theme. Cable TV, and the white-pebbled spa does water therapy!
Saigon-Phu Quoc, Tran Hung Dao St, tel: 77 384 6999, phuquocsales@hcm.vnn.vn www.vietnamphuquoc.com State-owned resort set in gardens on the beach. Modern look. Rooms have cable TV, safes, hairdryers – and magnifying mirrors.

MID-RANGE
Can Tho
Hoa Binh Hotel, 05 Hoa Binh Avenue, tel: 71 381 0218/9, hoabinhct@hcm.vnn.vn www.hoabinhct.com Newly refurbished centrally located hotel with Wi-Fi, TV, central controls, telephone, AC, tubs/showers, nice corner (counters) sink with hot water. Some splash showers.

Chau Doc
Chau Pho Hotel, 88 Trung Nu Vuong, tel: 76 356 4139, chauphohotel@vnn.vn www. chauphohotel.com Lift, cable TV, tubs and showers with hot water, telephones, even slip-pers. Very reasonably priced.

My Tho
Chuong Duong Hotel, 10 D 30/4 Street, tel: 73 387 0875, vietcdtourist@yahoo.com.vn Great location by the river.
Hoa Binh Hotel, 5 Hoa Binh, tel: 71 381 0218/9, hoabinh ct@hcm.vnn.vn Renovated and good value.

Long Xuyen
Dong Xuyen, 9A Luong Van Cu, tel: 76 394 2260, dong xuyenag@hcm.vnn.vn Huge hotel; jacuzzi, sauna and com-fortable rooms. Good value.
Hang Chau, 10 Nguyen Van Thoai, tel: 76 386 8891. A good small hotel with satellite TV and air-conditioning.

Phu Quoc Island
Cassia Cottage Phu Quoc, Tran Hung Dao St., tel: 77 384 8395, cassiacottage@ cassiacottage.com Cottages of various sizes, in tropical gardens around a pool, Wi-Fi, AC and fans. Very good value.

BUDGET
Can Tho
Hotel Xuan Mai, 94 Nguyen An Ninh Street, tel: 71 381 5217, www.xuanmaihotel. com.vn Central mini-hotel with lift. Modern, low rates.

The Mekong Delta and Phu Quoc Island at a Glance

Chau Doc
Thanh Nam 2, 10 Quang Trung, tel: 76 321 2616, thanhnamhotel@yahoo.com www.hotels-chaudoc.com This light new mini-hotel offers AC, hot splash showers and cable TV. Good value.
Thuan Loi Hotel, 18 D Tran Hung Dao, tel: 76 386 6134. Good budget hotel on the river, with floating restaurant.

Rach Gia
Phuong Hoang Hotel, 6 Nguyen Trung Truc, tel: 77 386 6525. Air conditioning, hot water, TV and fridge.

Phu Quoc Island
Tropicana Resort Phu Quoc, Tran Hung Dao, tel: 77 384 7127, tropicana_vn@yahoo. com www.tropicanavietnam. com Comfortable rooms with phones, cable TV. Free internet. The beach is 100m down the lane. Very charming.
Sea Star Resort, Ba Keo, 7 ward, Tran Hung Dao St, tel: 77 398 2161, phuquocsea star@yahoo.com www.seastar resort.com Bungalows have AC, cable TV, and hot showers. There's no pool, but it's situated on the beach.
Thousand Stars Resort (Ngan Sao), Tran Hung Dao, tel: 77 384 8203, www.ngansao resort-phuquoc.com.vn Somewhat eccentric resort offering pleasant AC rooms in beach bungalows and two-storey blocks. Huge pool.
Kim Nam Phuong, 88/5 Tran Hung Dao tel: 77 384 6319,

kimnamphuong.hotel@yahoo. com.vn www.hotels-phuquoc. com Simple bungalows, several with sea view. Hot water splash showers, cable TV.
Thanh Hai Bungalow, 118/2 Tran Hung Dao Street, tel: 77 384 7482, thanhhairesort@ yahoo.com Simple bungalows with hot water splash showers, AC or fan, and terraces with hammocks.
Beach Club, Tran Hung Dao Street, tel: 77 398 0998, info@beachclubvietnam.com www.beachclubvietnam.com Thatched bungalows with bamboo beds, hot splash showers, two chairs and a table. Very rustic.

WHERE TO EAT

My Tho
My Tho's speciality is *hu tieu my tho*, spicy noodle soup, seafood, pork and chicken.
Chuong Duong Restaurant, tel: 93 397 0322.

Can Tho
If you're game, the specialty here is *ran* – snake fried in curry.
Thien Hoa Restaurant, tel: 71 382 1942, and **Nambo Restaurant**, tel: 71 382 3908, both in Hai Ba Trung Street.

Chau Doc
The specialty is *canh chua ca* – a sweet 'n sour fish soup.
Dong Que, Duong Trung Nu Vuong, tel: 76 356 0057. The stonework of this open wooden pavilion are hung with pots of orchids. Try the huge steamed prawns, fresh from the river.
Co May, Trung Nu Vuong, tel: 76 356 4054. This place, recommended by locals, specializes in fish and seafood.

Rach Gia
Known for its dried seafood and *nuoc mam* fish sauce.
Hoa Bien Restaurant, Nguyen Hung Son, tel: 77 392 9797. Seafood.

TOURS AND EXCURSIONS

See Getting There, previous page. In Phu Quoc, English-speaking **Tony's Snorkeling Tours** (100 Tran Hung Dao, tel: 84 0913 820 714, info@ tonyanh.com or anhtupq@ yahoo.com www.discover phuquoc.com) does snorkeling and fishing tours to the islands in the south as well as night time squid fishing.
Dongnoi-Phuquoc Tourist, tel: 77 399 4444, leads treks through the jungle.

MEKONG DELTA	J	F	M	A	M	J	J	A	S	O	N	D
AVERAGE TEMP. °F	77	79	81	84	83	80	81	81	81	81	81	78
AVERAGE TEMP. °C	25	26	27	29	28	27	27	27	27	27	27	26
RAINFALL in	0	0	0	2	7	8	9	8.5	11	11	6	2
RAINFALL mm	12	22	10	50	177	206	227	217	273	277	155	41
DAYS OF RAINFALL	2	1	1	3	14	17	18	18	19	18	11	5

Travel Tips

Tourist Information

Vietnam Tourism in Hanoi and Ho Chi Minh City and **Saigon Tourist** in Ho Chi Minh City are two large, state-run organizations that deal with practicalities like visa extensions, and offer organized tours and valuable tourist information. Tourist offices in other parts of the country, many privately owned and cheaper than their state-run counterparts, are listed in the 'At a Glance' section of the relevant chapters.

Getting There

By air: More than 40 international airlines now fly into Vietnam, as well as the new budget carriers: Air Asia, Jetstar, Lion Air, Nok Air, Pacific Airlines and Tiger Airlines. From **Europe**: Some 20 airlines fly to Vietnam, not all non-stop. Those offering the lowest fares use Bangkok, Kuala Lumpur and Singapore as hubs, then a budget airline booked separately on to Hanoi or HCMC. From **Australia**: Cathay Pacific, China Airlines, China Southern Airlines, Jetstar, Malaysian Airlines, Singapore Airlines and Thai Airways connect numerous towns in Australia with Ho Chi Minh City. From the **USA**: American, Asiana, Cathay Pacific, Continental, Delta, Dragonair, EVA, Japan Airlines,

Korean Air, Shanghai Airlines and Vietnam Airlines have flights from both East and West Coasts.

By land: From Cambodia there are border crossings at Moc Bai-Bavet, by bus, at Vinh Xuong-Kaam Samnor by boat (from Phnom Penh), at Xa Xia-Prek Chak in the Mekong Delta, or a fast, more expensive boat run by Victoria Hotels (www.victoriahotels-asia.com) from Chau Doc to Phnom Penh. Also Pandaw Cruises run boats from Ho Chi Minh City to Siem Reap (www.pandaw.com). A cheaper option is Toum Teav Cruises (www.cfmekong.com). There is also a crossing at Le Thanh O Yadaw in Vietnam's remote northwest. For hearty travellers, to or from China, there are three border crossings for foreigners: Friendship Pass at Dong Dang 164km northeast of Hanoi, Lao Cai and Mong Cai (must arrange Chinese or Vietnamese visas in advance). From Laos, there are seven border crossings, the most popular being Lao-Bao-Dansavanh linking Dong Ha and Savannakhet. That at Cau Treo-Nam Phao beween Hanoi and Vientiane is recommended as the journey from hell. Crossing at Nam Can-Nong Haet, buses connect Vinh and Ponsavan and the Plain of Jars. There is a little-

used crossing at the Cha Lo-Na Phao linking Dong Hoi and Tha Khaek, and remote crossings at Na Meo-Nam Xoi which connects Thanh Hoa south of Hanoi with Xam Nua and one at Bo Y-Phou Keau linking Quy Nhon and Kon Tum in the south with Attapeu and Pakse. The most recent border crossing to open is at Tay Trang-Sop Hun connecting Dien Bien Phu and Muang Khua.

By train: Trains run from Hanoi to Beijing three times weekly. The 1770 mile (2950km) trip takes 48hrs. Trains run from Hanoi to Kunming in China, 567 miles (762km) via Lao Cai.

By sea: The occasional cruise ship calls in at Vietnamese ports. Check out the latest options and availability with your local travel agency.

Airport Tax

Airlines now include the departure tax in the price of tickets. NOTE: On some domestic flights, Vietnam Airlines insists on weighing carry-on bags, which can result in paying overweight.

Entry Requirements

All visitors must have a valid passport stamped with a visa issued by a **Vietnamese embassy**. Time needed to process a visa application varies from embassy to embassy – expect 1–2 weeks. Bangkok is the quickest and easiest place to obtain a visa. Tourist visas are normally valid for 30 days and can be extended in Vietnam for a further 30 days by major travel agents or at an Immigration Police Office (fee is usually around US$20–25). Re-entry visas are required should the traveller exit Vietnam to, for example, Cambodia, and then return. Travel agents in Vietnam can arrange re-entry visas. There are also three-month multiple entry tourist visas, which are extendable.

Customs

You do not need to declare jewellery or electronic goods for your own personal use, but you must keep the customs slip attached to your passport on entry to be shown at departure. There is a **Duty Free Allowance** of 200 cigarettes or 50 cigars or 250g of tobacco, 1 litre of spirits and 1 litre of wine, along with a 'reasonable' amount of personal effects. Export of some items is restricted. This includes antiques, which may be confiscated on departure – enquire about restrictions when purchasing (but there is no guarantee).

Health Requirements

It is advisable, but not obligatory, to be vaccinated against cholera, typhoid, polio, tetanus and hepatitis. A basic medical kit should include anti-malaria tablets and strong anti-diarrhoea medicine. Avoid dogs to avoid rabies. Don't drink tap water and only eat raw fruit or vegetables in reputable restaurants. Medical standards in Vietnam, especially outside Hanoi and Ho Chi Minh City, are much lower than those in more developed countries. Greater care should be taken with hygiene, particularly in rural areas. If major medical care becomes necessary, it is best to fly to Bangkok, Singapore or Hong Kong.

Security

Pickpockets and touts are a problem, especially in Ho Chi Minh City and Nha Trang. Otherwise, streets are generally safe. As always when travelling, watchfulness and commonsense precautions should prevail. Undetonated explosives can still be a danger in some rural areas where there was heavy fighting during the war. Keep to pathways.

What to Pack

The Vietnamese tend to dress simply and informally, both sexes favouring shirts and long trousers. While suits and ties are rarely worn, a clean, neat appearance is particularly appreciated. Shabbily and scantily dressed travellers are likely to be poorly treated. Light, natural fabrics are the most comfortable, but jumpers and coats are recommended in the north during the winter months. A sun hat in summer is useful, as is beachwear for the coastal resorts.

Accommodation

Outside of Hanoi and Ho Chi Minh City, hotels can be well below international standard, although choice and quality are improving with the rapid growth of new hotels being built throughout the country. Accommodation is quite comfortable, even in budget establishments, hot water is available everywhere, with the idiosyncracy that Vietnamese-style showers sometimes splash the entire bathroom. Many hotels have a variety of room categories (and prices) depending on furnishing and the availability or otherwise of air conditioning. For details of recommended establishments, consult 'At a Glance' sections at the end of each chapter.

Transport

Air: Vietnam Airlines operates flights to Buon Ma Thuot, Da Lat, Da Nang, Hai Phong, Hue, Na San, Nha Trang, Pleiku, Qui Nhon, Phu Quoc Islands, Vinh, Hue, Tuy Hoa, Rach Gia, Con Son and Dien Bien Phu. The budget airline Jetstar now serves Hanoi, Haiphong, Vinh, Hue, Danang, Nha Trang and HCMC.

Train: A rail service operates between Hanoi and Ho Chi Minh City via Hue, Da Nang and Nha Trang. The complete journey takes from 30 to 41hrs. Train travel in Vietnam, even first class, is recommended for the adventurous only. New rail cars with air-conditioned sleeping berths and dining cars are now available on 'express' trains, but 'express' still means 30hrs from Hanoi to Ho Chi

Minh City. It is, nonetheless, an interesting experience.

Bus: 'Sleeper' buses operated by the travel cafés run the length of Vietnam.

Hire car: Car with driver (there are as yet no self-drive rentals) is the most comfortable and convenient way to travel and is comparatively inexpensive. The state of most roads, even Highway 1, which has been much improved, remains lumpy in places, while the general standard of driving is erratic. Buses and motorbikes make up most of the traffic.

Money Matters

Currency: The dong is the official currency. It is issued in banknotes only in denominations of 200, 500, 1000, 2000, 5000, 10,000, 20,000 and 50,000.

Currency exchange: The rate of exchange fluctuates around 19,000 dong to US$1. US dollars are widely accepted – large-denomination notes get better rate of exchange, but a supply of small bills should be kept for tips, etc. Hotel reception counters also change money, usually at a fair rate. Most cities offer abundant ATMs. Travellers' cheques (best in US$) can be exchanged in major cities.

Credit cards: Visa and Mastercharge cards are accepted throughout the country in luxury establishments, but smaller establishments demand payment in cash.

Banks: Banking hours are Monday to Friday (08:00–11:30 and 13:00–16:00) and on Saturdays (08:00–11:30).

ATMs: Vietcombank has the largest network throughout the country. Withdrawals in dongs but withdrawals in dollars can be arranged over the counter.

Tipping: Tipping is not expected, nor is it refused. International hotels and restaurants normally add a five to 10 per cent service charge to bills. It is customary to tip guides and drivers, or in buses to collect a communal tip.

Business Hours

Government and most other offices work from Mondays to Saturdays (07:30–16:30). Lunch breaks vary from 1–2hr.

Shops tend to stay open late. Nightspots close at around 23:00–23:30.

Time Difference

Vietnam is 7hr ahead of GMT.

Communications

In addition to GPOs in Hanoi and Ho Chi Minh City, major hotels offer postal, telex, fax and e-mail services. Mail can take two weeks or more to reach its destination. It is better to give outgoing mail to a departing traveller to post overseas. Leading Ho Chi Minh City hotels have IDD telephone facilities. IDD and faxes are expensive, so e-mail is the best form of communication. Internet shops are plentiful.

Electricity

Most electric current is 220V/50 cycles, but 110V is also found, especially in rural areas. Beware of power surges which can affect computers and other electrical appliances. Two-pin plugs are usual, but some are flat and some round and so a multi-adapter is useful.

Etiquette

Most people are friendly and hospitable. In rural areas and among children especially, curiosity is often so great as to seem intentionally rude – it is not. Understanding and patience are necessary. Also, offence should not be taken at direct personal questions – one's age, income, etc. In official dealings red tape is everywhere, again, patience combined with perseverance is required. Avoid shouting,

CONVERSION CHART		
FROM	**TO**	**MULTIPLY BY**
Millimetres	Inches	0.0394
Metres	Yards	1.0936
Metres	Feet	3.281
Kilometres	Miles	0.6214
Square kilometres	Square miles	0.386
Hectares	Acres	2.471
Litres	Pints	1.760
Kilograms	Pounds	2.205
Tonnes	Tons	0.984
To convert Celsius to Fahrenheit: x 9 ÷ 5 + 32		

USEFUL VIETNAMESE PHRASES

Greetings
Hello/goodbye •
Chao (formal to older
man/woman)
• *Chao ong/ba*
(less formal)
• *Chao anh/chi*
How are you?
• *(Ong/ba* or
anh/chi)
Co khoe khong?
Fine, thanks.
• *Cam on (ong/ba)*
toi van thuong.
What is your name?
• *Ten (ong/ba* or
ang/chi) la gi?
My name is…
• *Ten toi la…*
Good night
• *Chuc ngu ngon*

Useful questions
How much is it?
• *Bao nhieu?*
Where is the…?
• …*o dau?*

**Useful words and
phrases**
Yes/No • *Co/Khong*
Thank you • *Cam on*
I don't understand.
• *Toi khong hieu.*
I want/need • *Toi can*

I don't want •
Toi khong can
I like • *Toi thich*
I don't like •
Toi khong thich
I'm hungry • *Toi doi*
I'm very thirsty
• *Toi khat lam*
I'm unwell
• *Toi bi benh*

Other useful words
Bathroom • *Nha tam*
Bus • *Xe buyt*
Bus station • *Ben xe*
Cheap • *Re*
Chemist • *Nha thuoc*
Cyclo • *Xe xich-lo*
Doctor • *Bac si*
Expensive • *Dat*
Hospital • *Benh vien*
Hotel • *Khach san*
Hot water • *Nuoc
nong*
Market • *Cho*
Mountain • *Nui*
Post office • *Buu dien*
River • *Song*
Restaurant • *Nha
hang*
Telephone • *Dien
thoai*
Toilet • *Nha ve sinh*
Train station •
Ga xe lua

Food and drink
Water • *Nuoc*
Drinking water
• *Nuoc uong*
Tea • *Nuoc che*
(north), *Nuoc tra*
(south)
Coffee • *Ca phe*
Sugar • *Duong*
Beer • *Bia*
Apple • *Bom tao*
Banana • *Trai chuoi*
Beef • *Thit bo*
Butter • *Bo*
Chicken • *Thit ga*
Durian • *Trai sau
rieng*
Fish • *Ca*
Lemon • *Chanh*
Orange • *Trai cam*
Oyster • *So*
Papaya • *Trai du du*
Shrimp • *Tom*
Vegetables • *Rau*
White rice • *Com
trang*

Days of the week
Monday • *Thu hai*
Tuesday • *Thu ba*
Wednesday • *Thu tu*
Thursday •*Thu nam*
Friday • *Thu sau*
Saturday • *Thu bay*
Sunday • *Chu nhat*

Yesterday • *Hom qua*
Today • *Hom nai*
Tomorrow • *Ngay mai*
Morning • *Sang*
Evening • *Chieu*

Numbers
One • *Mot*
Two • *Hai*
Three • *Ba*
Four • *Bon*
Five • *Nam*
Six • *Sau*
Seven • *Bay*
Eight • *Tam*
Nine • *Chin*
Ten • *Muoi* or *chuc*
Eleven • *Muoi mot*
Twelve • *Muoi hai*
Twenty • *Hai muoi*
Twenty-one
• *Hai muoi mot*
Thirty • *Ba muoi*
One hundred
• *Mot tram*
Two hundred
• *Hai tram*
One thousand
• *Mot nghin*
Ten thousand
• *Muoi nghin*
One hundred thou-
sand • *Tram nghin*
One million •
Mot trieu

argument or displays of anger.
It is common courtesy to ask
permission before taking someone's picture. Shyness can lead
to awkward situations and
some tribal minorities may
object to being photographed.
The Vietnamese appreciate
politeness, good manners and
correct dress. The correct form
of address is the relevant prefix

(Mr, Madame, Miss) followed
by the given name. Vietnamese
people normally have three
names: first the family name,
followed by a middle name
and lastly the given name.

Festivals and Holidays

Traditional festivals remain an
essential part of the culture,
their celebration illustrative

of the typical Vietnamese character and identity. The most
important annual festivity is the
Lunar New Year, while other
events also follow the lunar
calendar. Several holidays have
been added to the list of celeb-
rations influenced by Chinese
religious culture. The important
events and public holidays are
listed overleaf.

1 January: Western New Year's Day.

Late January/Early February: Tet (Tet Nguyen Dan, meaning 'first morning of the new period') – the Lunar New Year and the beginning of spring celebrated from the first to the seventh day of the first lunar month. Probably the biggest celebration of the year.

3 February: The Founding of the Communist Party of Vietnam in 1930.

March: Hai Ba Trung Day – celebrates the Trung sisters, who led a revolt against the Chinese in AD39 that held out for two years. After being defeated, the sisters committed suicide. Celebrated on the 6th day of the 2nd lunar month.

April: Thanh Minh – a festival honouring the dead, the 5th or 6th day of the 3rd lunar month.

30 April: Liberation Day – celebrates the anniversary of the day Ho Chi Minh City (Saigon) surrendered to the North Vietnamese Army.

1 May: Labour Day.

19 May: The anniversary of Ho Chi Minh's birth in the northern province of Nghe Tinh in 1890.

May/June: Anniversary of the Buddha – celebrates his birth, enlightenment and death.

August: Trung Nguyen (Wandering Souls' Day) – the 15th day of the seventh lunar month marks the important festival of remembrance of the dead, with prayers and offerings to absolve sins.

2 September: National Day – commemorates Ho Chi Minh's proclamation of independence in 1945.

3 September: Ho Chi Minh's Anniversary – commemorates his death in 1969.

September/October: Trung Thu (Mid-Autumn Festival) is on the 15th day of the eighth lunar month. Traditional features of the festival are rice moon cakes and decorated, brightly coloured lanterns.

November: Confucius's birthday – celebrated on 28th day of the ninth month.

25 December: Christmas Day (not an official holiday).

Language

Tonal and monosyllabic, Vietnamese is a difficult language for Westerners to master. Five tones are used in the south, six in the north, and every syllable is inflected by a tone, which determines the meaning. Thus words sounding the same to an untrained ear may have five (or six) different meanings. French is only spoken by the very old, while English is gaining in popularity. German and Russian are understood to a lesser extent, especially in the south. The language barrier can be a problem and although foreigners can muddle through, a few Vietnamese words can be useful and courteous. Bilingual dictionaries (English–Vietnamese and Vietnamese–English) are easily obtainable in Ho Chi Minh City and Hanoi and, for the more ambitious, courses in the language are run in Ho Chi Minh City and Hanoi.

GOOD READING

Borton, Lady (1995) *After Sorrow: An American among the Vietnamese.* A moving account of an American woman's experiences when she shares the life of two villages, North and South, in the 90s. New York.

Duong Thu Huong (2000) *Memories of a Pure Spring.* A fictional account of how a singer and her composer husband struggle to survive in modern Vietnam. Picador, New York.

Fitzgerald, Francis (1972) *Fire in the Lake.* Multiple prize-winning account of US involvement in Vietnam.New York.

Greene, Graham *The Quiet American* (1955). A classic and prophetic modern novel of Vietnam at the end of the French conflict and the beginning of American involvement. London.

Herr, Michael (1977) *Dispatches.* A superbly readable 'new journalism' account of the war. New York.

Huu Ngoc (1997) *Sketches for a Portrait of Vietnamese Culture.* An in-depth analysis of how Vietnam's history and literature have shaped the nation. The Gioi Publishers, Hanoi.

Lewis, Norman (1951) *Dragon Apparent.* One of the best travel books on Vietnam – a classic. London.

Sheehan, Neil (1988) *A Bright Shining Lie: John Paul Vann and Americans in Vietnam.* A highly acclaimed biographical account of the USA and the war; Pulitzer and National Book Award winner. New York.

INDEX